THE

MAKING OF AMERICA

SERIES

WATERTOWN

A HISTORY

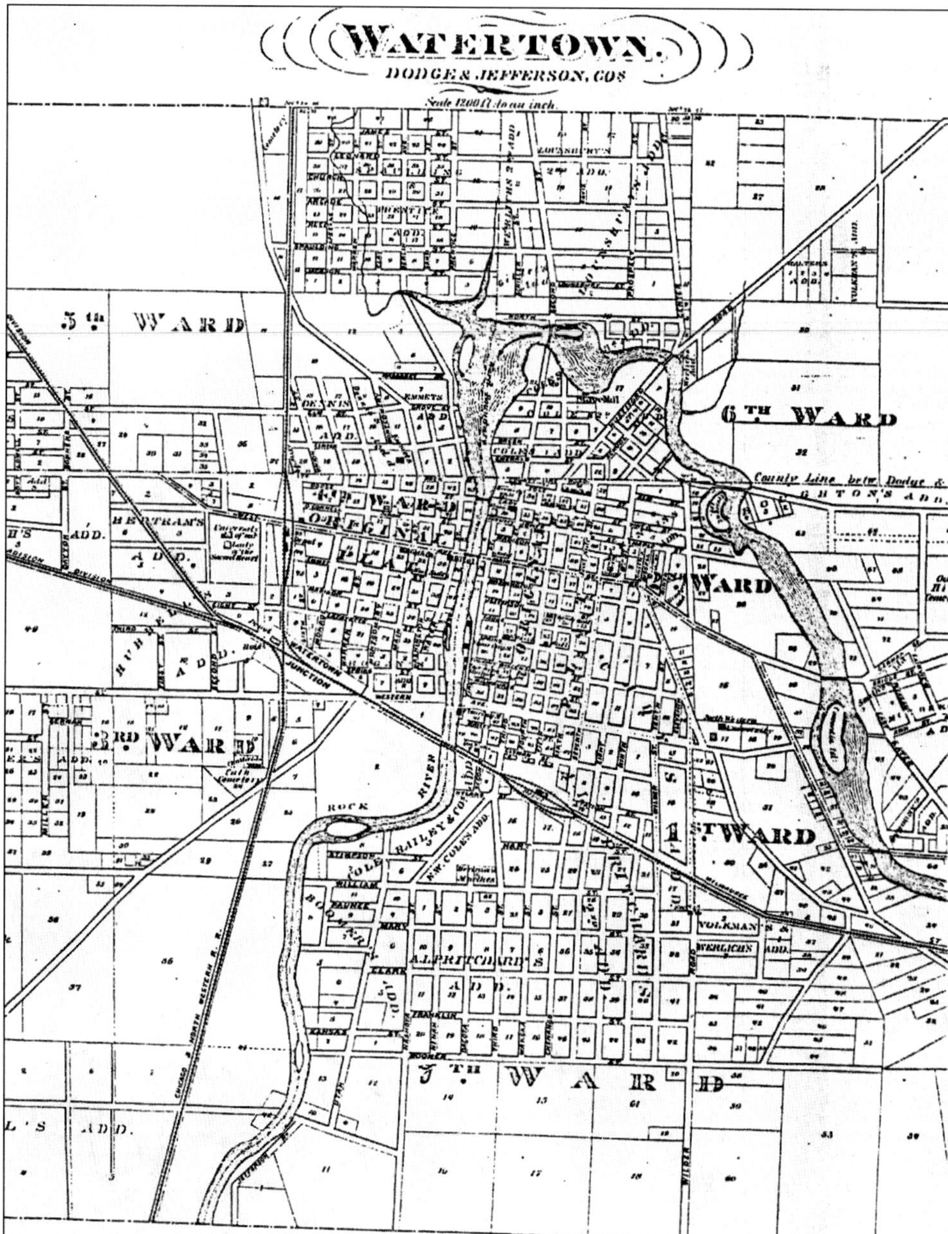

PLAT OF WATERTOWN. This plat map of Watertown, Wisconsin shows the town as it appeared c. 1890.

THE

MAKING OF AMERICA

SERIES

WATERTOWN

A HISTORY

W.F. JANNKE III

ARCADIA
PUBLISHING

ISBN 978-0-7385-2392-7

Published by Arcadia Publishing
Charleston, South Carolina

Printed in the United States of America

Library of Congress Catalog Card Number: 2002108719

For all general information contact Arcadia Publishing at:
Telephone 843-853-2070
Fax 843-853-0044
E-Mail sales@arcadiapublishing.com
For customer service and orders:
Toll-Free 1-888-313-2665

Visit us on the Internet at www.arcadiapublishing.com

THE MUTUAL BASEBALL TEAM. This was Watertown's leading team in the 1880s. (Gerald Kreitzman collection.)

Contents

ACKNOWLEDGMENTS

No one creates a work such as this alone and so the author would like to express his thanks to the following individuals and historical societies for their assistance in creating this book:

The Watertown Daily Times, Thomas Schultz, Bernhard and the late Eleanore (Nack) Schroeder, the late Charles Wallman, Frank and Georgianne Lindemann, John Reichardt, Jim Tobalske, Arline Hildebrandt, the Watertown Historical Society, Gerald Kreitzman, Lloyd Schultz, Sandra Haseleu, Judy Klein, Herman and Mary Rohr, Ken Riedl, Bethesda Lutheran Home, Yvonne Duesterhoeft, Edward Stuebe, and Debra Moralez.

I dedicate this volume of Watertown history to the memory of
my parents,
William F. and Phyllis (Jacobs) Jannke.

Foreword

Turn back the calendar, invert the hour-glass and let the sands of conquering time flow backward. Put aside thoughts of present trying times and journey back . . . to a Watertown of another era, a Watertown whose days and nights [were] spent in hard, careful work and simple homely entertainment. Step away from the era of the automobile, the radio . . . the airplane, the motion picture and stroll down the road of the past.

Watertown Daily Times, March 29, 1933

For years, I have yearned and dreamt of writing a history of Watertown—*the* history. Here, at last, is my first attempt at such a work. I have no illusions about this being *the* history of the city. This book, given its limited scope, merely scratches the surface. Nor do I wish to take anything away from others who have written about Watertown's rich past. Rather, I hope that this book will comfortably nestle somewhere between the more classic works, such as *Watertown Remembered* by the late E.C. Kiessling, and *Home Town* by the late Ralph David Blumenfeld. My hope is that I have done a creditable job of recording the history of my hometown. Time will tell.

Writing history is a lonely task and one that is often fraught with difficulties. Every source consulted seemed to contradict another in certain ways, and then there was the job of finding images to illustrate various points. But the hardest part was trying to maintain a delicate balance between stuffy academics and being entertaining. History can be deadly dull if it is not presented well. I hope I have added the right amount of color to make the story of Watertown palatable to even the most casual reader. Of course, books of this sort will really only appeal to residents, former residents, and history buffs, and they are the most demanding audience an author could hope to appease. There are several subjects that I have had to deal with in a brief manner or omit completely. This is troubling to me, since I love the many nuances of the city's history. Each night in my dreams these voices from the past kept crying out to me, begging me to tell their story, tell their story, but I have had to, in many cases, disappoint them.

I have deliberately set out not to dwell on the darker aspects of the city's history. Most cities the size of Watertown have had a seamier side, but this is not the book for that sort of thing. Rather, I have chosen to emphasize the more

WHERE IS WATERTOWN? Watertown, Wisconsin is in the southeastern part of the state and rests comfortably between Madison, the state capital, and Milwaukee, the largest city in Wisconsin. It is a mere 45-minute drive from either city and is two hours from Chicago.

positive things about life in an atypical Midwestern city. I say atypical, for there is something about Watertown that is quite unlike any other place I have been to. We have our own way of doing things, even our own way of speech. The older citizens still speak with a sort of patois made up of New England idioms, sprinkled generously with German sentence structure, and delivered in a nasally Midwestern twang. For example, where most people would say, "Why don't you come to my home and visit with me?", we in Watertown are more likely to say, "Vy don't youse come by der house onc't, n'so?" Or instead of saying, "I was all alone in the house," in Watertown you might hear, "I was by myself just in der house."

People still come to downtown Watertown for the twice-monthly Fair Day and buy fresh produce and flowers; they head for the Chalet or C.D. Beck's Restaurant for breakfast, Mullen's Dairy Bar for a soda or ice cream cone on warm summer days, and Zwieg's Grill or the Elias Inn for the regular Friday night fish fry. We believe in traditions and hold fast to them. Change doesn't come without a great deal of kicking and screaming. Yet, when it comes, being the naturally reticent German-heritage citizens that most of us are, we accept it quietly.

On Sundays, we go to church. At one time, there were two main religious factions, "der Lut'erns" (Lutherans) and "der Cat'lickers" (Catholics). The rich belonged to the "piscopal" (Episcopal) or Congregational churches. Other groups minded their own business. You were either a "west-sider" or an "east-sider" and that is what distinguished you in society at one time. I was a dyed-in-the wool west-sider. My father's people were from the "settlements," that area of town located at the western city limits. I grew up on the west side and it has only been fairly recently that I have been living on the east side. I still find it hard to reconcile my feelings about that.

I have seen changes in my hometown. We have grown from a city with approximately 12,000 people in my youth to the present city of nearly 22,000. However, despite the changes, I would like to think that our overall character is still in place. Ralph David Blumenfeld, a former Watertowner who rose to become the editor of the *London Daily Express*, wrote a delightful book in 1944 entitled *Home Town*, which was about his childhood in Watertown. In his book he wrote, "I first began to perceive that my home town was a thing apart, that it did things which were not done or thought of in other communities . . . it was a proud heritage to be a native of Watertown."

And I echo his sentiments entirely.

W.F. Jannke III

MAIN STREET. This photograph shows downtown Watertown, c. *1885.*

1. Pre-History

Come near, ye nations, to hear, and harken ye people; let the earth hear and all that is therein; for it came to pass in the year 1835 that a hardy band of Green Mountain boys left the land of their fathers, and journeyed west-ward toward the setting sun, even unto the great river which was known in those days as Sin Soepe, but in modern times is called Rock River. There on the banks of the river, they laid the foundation for a great city, which they called Watertown.

Watertown Chronicle, March 7, 1855

From the very beginning, the Rock River Valley attracted people, first Native Americans, then "Green Mountain boys" or Yankees. Following close on the heels of these two groups came the vast out-pouring of European countries, which have given this area its unique ethnic flavor. But if we wish to seek out the beginnings of Watertown, Wisconsin, we must go back through the mists of time to an era in which Europeans had not yet set foot on the banks of the Rock River, to the time of "the forest primeval."

The area's first inhabitants were known as Paleo-Native Americans and they may have arrived in the Watertown area as early as 12,000 years ago. At that time, Wisconsin's climate was much colder than it is today and glaciers covered much of the present state. As the glaciers began to recede, much of the area was covered with tundra vegetation. Animals, such as mammoths, mastodons, musk oxen, caribou, and large-toothed beavers, roamed the land. These animals provided food and clothing for the early inhabitants of what later became Wisconsin.

Following the Paleo-Native Americans came several periods identified by archaeologists, including the Archaic Period, which lasted from about 8500 B.C. to about 1000 B.C.; the Woodland Period, which began about 1000 B.C. and lasted 2,300 years; the Mississippian Period and Oneota Period, which followed the Woodland Period and lasted until the arrival of European settlers.

What was the lifestyle of these early people? Judging from recent archaeological discoveries, it would appear that people living here during the Archaic Period were semi-nomadic and lived in semi-permanent seasonal villages. They engaged in limited agriculture and used the bow and arrow for hunting and defending themselves. The Woodland Period saw the further development of Native

POTTAWATOMIE AND WINNEBAGO (HO CHUNK) INDIAN BRAVES. Native Americans like these were the Watertown area's earliest inhabitants.

American life. Villages grew larger and societies became more complex. The Woodland people were credited with making the first pottery in Wisconsin. They also created intricate fish weirs, used to direct fish into shallow areas where they would be easier to catch. Many of these ancient weirs still exist in the Watertown area.

The two Native American tribes most associated with Watertown's earliest history were the Pottawatomie and Winnebago (now called Ho-Chunk) tribes. The Ho-Chunk began to arrive in Wisconsin in the 1600s and had migrated to the Watertown area by the early 1700s, settling on the west side of the Rock River in what is today Watertown by 1735. The Ho-Chunk wore clothing typically made of tanned hides, mostly made from deerskins and richly decorated with porcupine quills. Men of the tribe wore breechcloth, leggings, moccasins, and in cold weather, buckskin robes and fur turbans. Women wore sleeveless dresses made from deerskin, with buckskin leggings, and their hair was usually braided.

A BIRCH-BARK NATIVE AMERICAN DWELLING. The Woodland Indians in the Watertown area lived in homes much like this in the eighteenth and nineteenth centuries.

The men of the Ho-Chunk occupied themselves in woodworking, creating bows and arrows, spears, lures, sleds, canoes, and other items. The women worked with birch bark and made baskets of sweet grass. They also tanned hides and wove reed mats.

Upon settling here, the Ho-Chunk continued to live in much the same way they always had. The new surroundings were rich in resources, such as fish, wild rice, shellfish, small game, and waterfowl. They also found that crops grew well in the fertile soil. The tribe still moved seasonally, leaving their summer villages in order to trap animals for their pelts in the winter. This trait they shared with their neighbors on the east side of the Rock River, the Pottawatomies.

The Pottawatomie were the second major Native American tribe to settle in the Watertown area. Their original home was probably in eastern Michigan, but due to the expanding power of other tribes, they began to migrate first to the eastern shore of Lake Michigan and then north to Saul Ste. Marie. By the 1640s, they had come into Wisconsin. Here they thrived and began to outnumber other tribes. The Pottawatomies arrived in what is now Watertown by 1722 and settled on the eastern shore of the Rock River.

Relations between the two tribes were apparently amicable. Even their earliest dealings with white settlers were without incident. But that would later change.

The first Europeans to arrive in Wisconsin were Jesuit missionaries sent from France to "civilize the savages." They were followed in short order by French fur traders who saw the potential value in animal pelts, especially the pelt of the beaver, for use in hat making.

It is nearly impossible to say for certain what traders were operating in what later became Watertown. Many traders chose to follow the "drouine" method of dealing with the Native American inhabitants of the area. This meant that instead of establishing a set trading post, such as the one belonging to Solomon Juneau in Milwaukee where Native Americans could bring pelts to the traders in exchange for goods, traders were compelled to travel to the various encampments to barter with tribal leaders and hunters directly. As a result, no one trader could be clearly identified with the Watertown area.

However, according to Timothy Johnson, Watertown's founder, and many others, there was a trader who had a cabin in what is now Watertown by the 1820s. Johnson discovered the ruins of this cabin on his first visit here in 1836. It was located in the southwestern part of the city. According to an apocryphal account related in the late nineteenth century, this trader's name was Monsieur Pierre La Belle and he was a favorite of all the tribes in this area. As the story goes, one day he was out boating on his favorite lake or "Lac," near what is now the city of Oconomowoc, when his canoe upset and he drowned. He was carried back to his

HATCHET FOUND IN ROCK RIVER. Artifacts like this are still found in Watertown, though somewhat infrequently. They are tangible reminders of the area's rich Native American heritage. (Watertown Historical Society collection.)

BLACK HAWK. This Sauk Indian chief brought his band of followers through what is today Watertown in July 1832.

cabin and buried by the local natives. A large cedar cross was erected over his grave and in his memory, the lake that he drowned in was named for him. Thus, today we find Lac LaBelle located east of Watertown in the Oconomowoc area. This all supposedly happened in 1827.

The fur trade lasted for many years, right up to the mid-1840s in some areas. Traders and the various Native American tribes worked peacefully together, each relying on the other for goods and services. The Pottawatomie in particular became dependent upon European trade goods, often forsaking their old ways in favor of the conveniences these goods gave them. But there was a drawback to this system. Apart from nearly obliterating the beaver from whole sections of the state due to over-harvesting them for their pelts, the white traders and settlers brought with them diseases, such as smallpox and cholera, which had never been seen before. The Native Americans in the area had no defenses against these scourges and, as a result, they began to die in great numbers. One estimate states that plagues such as these may have killed off 90 to 95 percent of the New World's native population.

White settlement began in earnest in the mid-1830s. The last Native American war in Wisconsin was the Black Hawk War, which was fought over broken promises and misunderstandings, and ultimately became a virtual purge of one Native American tribe. The war also served as a warning to any other tribe that might consider starting an uprising. With the termination of the Black Hawk War in 1832, the handwriting was on the wall for those Native Americans still remaining in southeastern Wisconsin. In 1832, the Ho-Chunk nation signed a treaty that deeded their land holdings west of the Rock River over to the United States government, followed by the Pottawatomie treaty of 1833 that deeded their land holdings east of the Rock River to the federal government in 1833.

Up to this point, we have been dealing in generalities. Let us now zero in on Watertown during this time. The Native American settlers of this area called this place Ka Ka Ree, which according to legend means "ox bow." They called it that because of the shape the Rock River makes as it winds its way through the city. Another source states that this area was also known as Grand Rapids, named, no doubt, for the rapids or falls that were present in the Rock River in the time before white settlers tamed it. There is a drop of 24 feet between the points where the Rock River enters the city and where it leaves the city limits. As E.C. Kiessling in his book *Watertown Remembered,* wrote:

BLACK HAWK MARKER. This sign, which overlooks the Rock River, tells the story of Black Hawk's passing through Watertown. It was erected in the late 1990s and is located along the River Walkway in downtown Watertown.

> As ancient Egypt was said to have been the gift of the Nile, so Watertown, in some respects, might have been called the gift of the Rock. Some miles to the east that lordly stream flows southward and would normally have missed Watertown. But then, as though it had over looked something precious, it turned back to the north and with a large endearing loop encircled the site of our city before flowing south to the Mississippi.

In 1836, United States government surveying teams were sent to the Wisconsin Territory to lay out township lines. One of these surveyors, John Mullet, reported that the land now encompassing Watertown "is rolling in places, lumbered with sugar (maple), lynn, elm, ironwood, maple, prickly ash, thorn, vines and oak." These trees would later provide new settlers with raw building materials.

There were several mounds or burial sites in the city, as well as a ceremonial spot on the west side where Maranatha Baptist Bible College is currently located. A local landmark that many early residents recalled was a Ho-Chunk hut near the Rock River bank along what is today East Division Street. This was, perhaps, the first permanent structure in Watertown. There were two tribal leaders or chiefs mentioned in connection with the area. One was Sea Sinker, who had a camp in nearby Aztalan, and the other was Iron Walker, who killed a French interpreter after a dispute over government payments in Baraboo, Wisconsin in 1836.

THE ROCK RIVER IN WATERTOWN. This photograph, taken in the 1890s, shows how the land in the Watertown area might have appeared to Native Americans and other early settlers.

ANOTHER VIEW OF THE RIVER. It was the power, the ease of transportation, and the abundance of fish in the waters of the Rock River that made this area so popular with both Native Americans and early Yankee settlers. (Watertown Historical Society collection.)

As previously stated, relations between whites and Native Americans were, for the most part, peaceful. Children of the early settlers liked to gather to watch the young braves shoot pennies off the tops of hitching posts with their bows and arrows. Some settlers, however, found the native population a nuisance. Women found them especially frightening. A favorite pastime of young braves was to press their faces against the windows of pioneer homes to scare the women. Eliza Richards, wife of the first attorney in Jefferson County and an early settler in Watertown, had an experience with a young Native American just after she arrived here in 1840 as a new bride. The story goes that she was baking bread in the kitchen of her home and when the brave came by, he smelled her bread baking and came into the cabin to ask her for some. Mrs. Richards, alone in the cabin and not wishing any trouble, readily gave the intruder all the bread she had made. Not long afterwards, this same brave returned with a decorated basket to pay her for her bread. This basket is still on exhibit at the Octagon House Museum in Watertown.

James Rogan, an early settler who arrived here in 1837, recalled years later that the Ho-Chunk were "the best neighbors I ever had. The Indians all liked me and my whisky." And this brings us to another facet of relations between white settlers and their Native American neighbors: liquor. White settlers often bartered with Native Americans, providing whiskey in exchange for goods like pelts or game. As a result, the natives here and elsewhere became dependent upon liquor. This often led to ugly disputes. Timothy Johnson recalled:

> In the spring of 1837, six drunken Indians and their squaws came to my log house and asked for whiskey, saying, in their native language, that they were "whiskey hungry." I refused to let them have any. This exasperated them, and one of their number, catching up an ax, aimed a blow at my head, but I warded it off, and jerking the ax from him, threw it some rods distance. I then seized a pitchfork, and striking him over the head, felled him to the ground.

The selling of liquor to area tribes was widespread. One of Johnson's sons sold whiskey to a young brave in exchange for a pony. Some dishonest settlers sold watered-down liquor, but most took perverse pride in telling people that they would never engage in so mean a trick as that, as if selling whiskey in its pure form was any more to be admired.

Sadly, as the years wore on, more and more Native Americans, it seemed, were reduced to petty thievery and ultimately became objects of pity and scorn. Timothy Johnson reported having a barrel of flour stolen from his home and James Rogan reported having a team of horses stolen by a band of Menomonee in 1839. In 1837, a Native American brave was accused of having stolen a watch from a white settler, as well as some mittens. He was promptly arrested and for his punishment, he was savagely whipped in front of his fellow tribesmen as a warning to future transgressors. The members of the whipping party were disappointed, however, when their victim didn't cry out and so they let him go.

In 1839, the first in a series of acts took place that would lead to the eventual removal of the Native American population from the Watertown area. Most of the Rock River band opted to leave the area just after the close of the Black Hawk War, and many moved north or to the middle of state. They had wanted to move at their own pace, but the sudden influx of white settlers demanded that they depart immediately, so they were forced out. As a result of the 1833 treaty, the Ho-Chunk were supposed to leave the area, but many didn't until much, much later. The government, after being inundated by complaints from settlers, stepped in and sent a team of "dragoons" to remove them by force. By 1841, the government began the actual removal process, but most of the Ho-Chunk soon came back again. In 1851, another systematic removal was undertaken, this time more successful, but as late as the 1880s, stray bands were sometimes seen in the area.

The Pottawatomie suffered a similar fate. The government in the early 1840s removed most, but a large number still lingered. In 1851, again at the request

THE INDIAN FOUNTAIN. *Erected in 1896, this fountain originally was placed in the middle of the intersection of Main and Washington Streets. It was knocked over in the 1920s and moved to Union Park and then to the grounds of the Octagon House Museum. This photograph from the 1940s shows the statue as it appeared in the park.*

of many citizens living along the Rock River, the government had this tribe removed as well. The Native Americans of this area did not go quietly. In 1837, for example, a rumor spread that a huge number of warriors were gathering and planning to swoop down on the whites that had settled in the Rock River Valley to drive them out. A similar scare arose in 1861. In each case, nothing came of the threat.

Perhaps the one Native American most people in Watertown were familiar with and interacted with on a daily basis was Dr. John Peter Quinney, a son of a Stockbridge chief. He came to Watertown in 1861 and resided at 500 Division Street where he hung out his shingle as an herbalist or botanical physician. He had a large herb garden in front of his home and from these various plants, he created poultices and potions, which cured ills from impotency to cancer. A prominent member of the Congregational church, he cut a distinctive figure amongst the people of the city. He usually wore a high silk hat, gold earrings, and often topped that off with a Native American blanket. He died in 1875 and is buried in Oak Hill Cemetery. When he died, all of the newspapers of the city mourned his passing and all agreed that he had a splendid character. They also agreed on one other point, that there was only one thing wrong with him: he was a Native American.

By the end of the nineteenth century, the former Indian tribes of the Watertown area were, for many, a distant memory. The few Native Americans that came through the area were looked upon with curiosity and pity. The Native American most people were familiar with in Watertown by this time was the fountain placed on Main Street in 1896 that depicted "A Noble Red Man." Knocked off his perch in 1923 and languishing in a city park for many years, this statue today can be found on the grounds of the Octagon House Museum in Watertown.

2. Pioneer Days: 1836–1840

At first the city progressed rather slowly; but as time rolled on, their brethren hearing of their whereabouts ventured forth into the wilderness; and yet others followed, until at last it was indeed a great city; and the whole city was of one language and one speech.

Watertown Chronicle, March 7, 1855

With the end of the last Indian war in Wisconsin in 1832, the land was thrown open to prospective settlers and many came to stake a claim in the newly opened territory. Starting in 1832, the federal government began to send out surveying teams to lay out the land in township lines.

Two of the many surveyors to see this area in its natural state were the team of Mullett and Brink. They had laid out township lines in 1834 and 1835. According to James Rogan, Watertown's pioneer Irish settler, Brink was very interested in settling here.

Rogan was at this time piloting a schooner, *The Grampus*, between Milwaukee and Cleveland. On one of his trips, he picked up the surveyor Brink and they began to talk of land prospects. Brink told Rogan of a wonderful spot he had just finished surveying. He spoke of the fine stands of timber and the beauty of the Rock River running through it all. Rogan, weary of life on the lakes, decided that he would stake a claim in this new place as soon as he was able.

He was not alone. Reports began to appear in east-coast newspapers that extolled the beauties of the Wisconsin Territory, and many adventurers left their homes to make a new life for themselves in the new west. One newspaper reported at this time that it seemed as though "the whole world is bound for the Rock River country." Among these was an itinerant carpenter with an incurable case of wanderlust named Timothy Johnson.

In January 1836, Johnson, late of Ohio, stepped off the stagecoach from Detroit. It had left him in Chicago and from there he went on foot to the city of Racine in the Wisconsin Territory where he met up with some friends. By January 16, he found himself in the southern part of the state where he met up with members of the Rock River Claim Company. This organization had been set up by various residents of Milwaukee in 1835 in order to look for possible mill sites along the Rock River.

CAPTAIN JAMES ROGAN. This image shows the earliest Irish settler in Watertown. A former captain on the Great Lakes, Rogan and his family came to Watertown in 1837. They were the second family to settle in the city. (Watertown Historical Society collection.)

Johnson tried to convince some of the members of the company to accompany him further up-river, but finding no takers, he went on alone. After making a few claims at various places in what is now Jefferson County, Wisconsin, he happened upon the future site of the city of Watertown in February 1836.

What sort of a man was this pioneer? There is but one photograph of him taken in the late 1850s. It shows a rather frail-looking sort of a man. He had a rudimentary education and judging from the only known letter written by him, which has recently come to light, he was possessed of a remarkable vocabulary, though only marginal spelling ability. He was a hearty sort of adventurer, used to walking long distances and also used to the solitary life of the explorer. A zealous Methodist exhorter, he provided his own home in which to hold the first church services in Watertown. Even after arriving in Watertown, he could not rest and, thus, his family found themselves being moved to a village a few miles to the south in 1838 that still bears his name, Johnson Creek. Then, in the early 1840s, he came back to Watertown, only to leave again in 1856. This time he went exploring in the northern part of the state. He returned to Watertown in 1863 and lived here until the end of the 1860s when illness forced his being sent to the state sanitarium where he died in 1871. He and his wife, Lucretia, the first white woman to settle in Watertown, lie side by side in Oak Hill Cemetery in Watertown.

Once this "Connecticut Yankee" arrived in what would become Watertown, he laid claim to 1,000 acres and named this new site Johnson's Rapids. His claim included the all-important water rights. In March of the same year, he brought two companions from the Rock River Claim Company, Reeve Griswold and Charles Seaton, back to his site and allowed them to enter quarter section claims.

The men then began to erect cabins for themselves. Johnson began to clear land for a home along what is today Milford Street in the southwestern part of the city. In late May, Johnson left the claim site to go into Milwaukee to buy some supplies. While he was gone, George Jarvis Goodhue and his brother-in-law Tyler Moore, settlers and land speculators at Beloit, Wisconsin, came up the Rock River looking for mill sites. They came upon the Watertown site and staked a claim. When Johnson returned, he could not get them to vacate so he settled for selling them his claim, including the water rights. Since this was before the time when land purchases could be made, no deeds were filed until 1839 when the land was put on the market. The selling price for this prime piece of real estate was reportedly a mere $100.

TIMOTHY JOHNSON, THE FOUNDER OF WATERTOWN. Johnson was a "Connecticut Yankee" who came to Wisconsin in 1835 and laid claim to the land encompassing the city of Watertown in the spring of 1836. (Watertown Historical Society collection.)

Leaving his cabin in a half-finished state, Johnson commenced building a small shanty located about where the North First Street parking lot is today. This was primarily for the benefit of the employees of the Goodhue Company, who were intent upon building a sawmill and dam at the Watertown site. The men began to arrive in late summer and started the erection of a dam across the river almost immediately, reportedly the first of its kind to be built on the Rock River in either Wisconsin or Illinois.

By the fall of 1836, there were about a dozen log cabins in the new settlement. At this time, Timothy Johnson sent for his family and set out for Milwaukee to meet them over a new road that he and several others had only recently opened. Upon arriving in Milwaukee, he found that his family had been waiting for two days for him. They left Milwaukee for Watertown on October 28 in the company of some men who had been hired to see them safely to the new settlement. The trip from Milwaukee to Watertown was filled with pitfalls and hardships, which resulted in the Johnson family not arriving in their new home until December 10.

As stated before, Lucretia (Brownell) Johnson was the first woman to arrive in Johnson's Rapids. Most of the men settling here at this time were young bachelors. She and her family were the first permanent residents of the newly created town. They spent their first Christmas in a small shanty, which was shared by them and several men working for the Goodhue Company. Thus, 1836 drew to a close.

LOG CABIN. The earliest settlers in Watertown erected dwellings such as this one. Once sawmills were established, frame houses became the norm and log cabins gradually faded from the landscape.

JOHNSON'S RAPIDS AS IT APPEARED IN 1837. This idealized view of the fledgling settlement was painted in the early 1900s.

The next year was filled with new adventures, new arrivals, and some sorrow. In December 1836, Luther A. Cole had arrived, as well as James Rogan, and they began to build homes for themselves. Cole, who along with his brother John would open the first retail store in the city in 1841, laid claim to land that sits in the Dodge County portion of the city, near what is today the Watertown Country Club. Here he kept a cabin with his brother John and fellow settler Amasa Hyland. John W. Cole did the household chores, though this is debatable, since according to Luther Cole's recollections, they made it their business not to wash the dishes until they could count the mouse tracks on them. The brothers referred to their cabin as a "bachelor's distress."

James Rogan had traded his schooner to Charles Seaton for his claims at Watertown in August and had installed his cook, Thomas Bass, to guard against claim jumpers. He brought his family to the new village in January 1837. The Rogan family was the second family to permanently settle here and was reportedly the first Irish family to settle in the city.

In February 1837, death came to the new village. Thomas Bass, James Rogan's former cook, was boarding with Charles Seaton and Ezra Dolliver in a small cabin located about where the Watertown Senior and Community Center is currently located, on South First Street. They had been drinking most of the day and after the last cup of grog was supped, they all passed out. Sometime over night, Bass decided to add more wood to the fire and, while doing so, he lost his balance and fell head first into the flames. The next morning his drinking companions discovered his charred remains.

The whole community attended his funeral and he was quickly buried. Word spread to Milwaukee, however, that someone had been killed and burned so a coroner's inquest was held. Seaton and Dolliver, initially thought by many to have killed Bass, were found innocent but soon fled the little community. Bass's remains were once more interred in an unmarked grave and all was forgotten. Until 1859.

That year, during some street work along South Third Street, a street crew accidentally came upon Bass's remains. Once again, his body was dug up and inspected and the saga of his death was discussed. He was then interred in old Oak Hill Cemetery and he was forgotten. Again. That is, until 1975.

In 1975, the city of Watertown condemned the old Oak Hill Cemetery property located along West Street on the southwest side of the city and sold the land to the Jehovah's Witness Congregation. Those still buried there were disinterred and removed to the present Oak Hill Cemetery on the east side of the city. One of those graves undoubtedly contained the skeletal remains of Thomas Bass. So you see, for a dead man, he was quite a traveler!

MRS. TIMOTHY JOHNSON. The former Lucretia Brownwell was the first white woman to settle in what is today Watertown. She died in 1857 and is buried alongside her husband in Oak Hill Cemetery. (Watertown Historical Society collection.)

LUTHER A. COLE. Cole arrived in Watertown at the end of 1836. Together with his brother John he founded the first retail store in the city in 1841. (Watertown Historical Society collection.)

The year 1837 saw a lot of firsts for Watertown: the first doctor arrived, Dr. J.R. Goodenough; the first frame house was erected by Bernard Crangle along Milford Street; and the first child was born in Watertown, believed to be Charles Johnson, a son of Timothy Johnson (though some sources claim the first birth was a daughter born to Isaac Hamison); the first German settler, Jacob Wedemann, arrived here; the first plow was brought to the village by James Rogan who also planted the first crops in this year; and the first lawyer arrived. This was John Richards, a native of Hinsdale, Massachusetts, who had walked here from his home on the east coast. By the spring of 1837, there were about 20 persons living in the area.

But 1837 also saw hard times for the country. A nationwide depression had settled in that caused banks to close and paper money to become worthless. Milwaukee prices went up dramatically and provisions grew scarce. A story from this time was widely told about the residents of Johnson's Rapids. It was claimed that the men couldn't take their shirts off to wash them because the amount of fish they consumed caused the bones to stick out of their bodies and hold their shirts fast to them. Fish became a staple since it was plentiful in the Rock River. James Rogan in his later years was fond of recalling that there were so many fish

JOHN W. COLE. A native of Vermont, John Cole rose from humble beginnings to become one of the richest men in Watertown, owning huge tracts of land, serving as mayor, and becoming a benefactor to the city. (Watertown Historical Society collection.)

in the river at this time that there were spots that wagons could cross the river on the backs of fish and the wagon wheels would never sink in the water. The lack of money and the hardships inherent in clearing the wilderness and carving out a new life caused many to abandon their claims and leave the area.

Still, there seemed to be something of permanence about the settlement and, in 1837, the first post office was established with William M. Dennis as the first postmaster. In his early days as postmaster, Dennis used to place the mail, carefully wrapped in a handkerchief, in his hat and carry it from place to place.

In May 1837, the Goodhue Company continued work on the dam and double sawmill, and by summer, the dam was finally completed. By December, the mill was up and running, which gave many residents employment. Milling, both sawmilling and flour milling, would be the major industry in Watertown throughout the nineteenth century. The lumber cut at the Goodhue mill was rafted down to Beloit and Rockford, Illinois via the Rock River. Lumber drifting down the river was a common sight throughout the 1850s. The next mill to be erected here would not come about until 1841 when Patrick Rogan built a sawmill on the west side of the river.

In the fall of 1837 a Methodist circuit rider, Reverend Jesse Halstead, arrived in the settlement and came to the home of Timothy Johnson. He was quite ill, but still managed to give a sermon, though he gave it from a chair. Afterwards, a collection was raised for him, but the money was for the most part made up of worthless paper currency. The cleric left the settlement just as poor as when he arrived. Johnson's Rapids was placed on the Aztalan Circuit and thus Methodist preachers came through the community regularly. This would be the only religious group to establish itself in Watertown until 1841 when Father Martin Kundig arrived and said the first Catholic Mass.

By the end of 1837, despite the depression and hardships, the number of residents in Johnson's Rapids was about 70, between 53 and 54 being adult males. There were about 10 or 12 log cabins in the town as well, most being hastily erected and roofed with shakes.

In 1838, the first reported school opened, taught by Miss Dolly Piper. The classroom was in a small building that was also used for town meetings and church services. Children living on the west side of the river had to canoe across in order to attend classes. The building was so small that when dancing was taught, legend has it the boys had to stand outside while the girls turned around.

WILLIAM M. DENNIS. This crayon portrait depicts Dennis late in life. He was one of the early movers and shakers in Watertown history, serving as the first postmaster in 1837 and later rising to the position of mayor. (Watertown Historical Society collection.)

In February 1839, the long awaited government land sales took place at Green Bay. Unlike other areas, which were at the mercy of land speculators that bid up choice pieces of land and then sold them at inflated prices, the citizens of Watertown and the surrounding area had protection from this practice by joining the Milwaukee Claim Organization in 1837. This organization helped look out for the small farmers and landowners and assured that everyone would get their land for the set price of $1.25 per acre. Also in 1839, Jefferson County was officially set off from Milwaukee County by legislative act. At the same time, the settlement changed its name from Johnson's Rapids to Watertown in honor of Watertown, New York where many settlers hailed from.

What did the little community look like at this time? Fortunately, Mrs. John W. Cole, the former Eliza Fisk, left her memories of the place at this time:

> I cannot convey to you in proper terms the mingled feelings of woe and disgust I entertained at my first sight of Johnson's Rapids. What could possess people to ever come to such a place was more than I could see. No sound to vibrate on the ear except the doleful noise of the saw-mill, and the general surroundings of the place were simply oppressive from my standpoint at the time.

But things were beginning to look up for the new town and the 1840s would bring new and exciting changes to this little Yankee settlement.

MRS. JOHN W. COLE IN 1895. The former Eliza Fisk was a formidable woman who didn't care too much for the rigors of pioneer life. Her greatest joy, besides her son Oscar, was to wear a full riding outfit and parade about the city on a white charger. (Watertown Historical Society collection.)

3. The Beginnings of a City: 1840–1850

And they said to one another, go to, and let us make brick, and burn them thoroughly—for their temples and all their buildings were made of oak and basswood; and they had brick for stone, and mud had they for mortar—and they built great temples and castles, some of brick, but mostly in air.

Watertown Chronicle, March 7, 1855

The 1840s were to be Watertown's turning point in many ways. True, it still had a ways to go as a village (which it would be declared in 1849), but the future looked bright. As the new decade began, there were little changes in the community. Some roads had been cleared, but the whole area still had a feeling of wilderness about it. A few cabins dotted the area, many of them built near the Rock River, but there was no definite Main Street or any retail outlets. Despite this seeming lack of progress, there was something in Watertown that brought people to the town and the population steadily rose throughout the 1840s.

The main industry to be found at this time was the sawmill, which was kept busy hewing timbers for new homes. The only other industry was farming and even that was not as strong as it would become since many found it more lucrative to work for the mills. Flour milling began about 1842 and a new market for farmer's crops opened. In 1841, the community suffered a major setback when the Goodhue mill burned to the ground, forcing many out of work. By 1842, however, the mill was back up and running again and by this time, other mills began to open in Watertown.

The first steps towards establishing permanence in Watertown came in 1840 when Edward and John C. Gilman erected a small hotel. This hotel, which was hastily finished in time for the first Fourth of July celebration in Watertown, was built on what would later become the northeast corner of Main and North First Streets. Called initially the Rock River Hotel, this establishment quickly became one of the busiest places in Watertown. It housed town meetings, lectures, and in 1844, it was the site of a dancing class taught to young people of the settlement. The Rock River Hotel spurred others on to open hotels of their own. The second

THE EXCHANGE HOTEL. This was the first building erected along what is today Main Street in downtown Watertown. It was built in 1840 by Isaac Savage for the Gilman brothers, John C. and Edward. It stood on the corner of Main and North First Streets. (Watertown Historical society collection.)

hotel to open in the city was located directly across the street from the Rock River Hotel and it was called the Planters. It opened in 1843. Other hotels that opened during this time period were the American House and the Farmer's Hotel. By the 1850s, Watertown was home to more than ten hotels or boarding houses, which, according to one historian, were filled to capacity on a daily basis.

The Rock River Hotel became known as the Exchange and in 1848, Jacob Bell Van Alstine, who was one of many colorful characters in Watertown's history, purchased it. Van Alstine was very fastidious about his place and saw to it that his hotel was kept clean. It was a never ending source of amusement to Watertown people to try to get the best of "Old Van of the Exchange." A popular trick was to wait until a heavy rain came and then run a pack of dogs with muddy feet into the front door of his hotel. Another story was told about a guest who came to the Exchange and asked for a room, but before he registered, he insisted upon inspecting it for cleanliness. Incensed, Van Alstine showed his guest the room and after being assured that it was clean to his liking, the guest declared he would take it, whereupon Van Alstine insisted upon checking the guest out to see if he was clean enough to sleep in his hotel!

The Exchange was a popular spot until the 1880s when Van Alstine died and, in 1892, the building was moved from Main Street to its present site, the corner of South First and Milwaukee Streets. It is currently a tavern and it has the distinction of being the oldest building in the city.

The first tentative steps towards retail development took place in the fall of 1841 when the Cole brothers, John and Luther, opened the very first general store in Watertown on the southwestern corner of Main and Second Streets. John W. Cole wrote the following to his brother in Vermont on March 30, 1842:

> We built us a store last fall and painted it in style . . . Business is very dull here at present. Western money is . . . worth only from 50 to 80 cents on the dollar, which makes it very bad for men that do much business. We bought about ten hundred dollars worth of goods last fall and we are owing about 50 dollars.

Prior to this, any goods that were needed had to be purchased in Milwaukee or as far way as Chicago, at exorbitant prices. With the opening of the Cole Brothers store, Watertown was placed on a much firmer footing. There was only one peculiar thing about this store: it was only open for business at night. During the day, the brothers were hard at work on their farm and they couldn't be bothered to open the store. Aside from that, the opening of this store marked the creation of the business district of Watertown.

THE PLANTERS HOTEL. This detail of an 1857 map of Watertown shows the second hotel to be built in Watertown. It was located on the southeastern corner of Main and South First Streets and burned to the ground in a spectacular blaze in 1868.

Main Street, or Bridge Street as it was known at this time, was not the first choice for commercial sites. When the city was laid out in blocks and streets it was determined that a better spot was in the southern part of the city along what is now Western Avenue. Accordingly, Western Avenue was created as a two-lane street, but before any retail stores could locate in this area of the city, greedy land speculators began to buy up lots facing the street and they jacked up the prices. No one could afford to locate there and so business people shifted the focus of their attention to the north and, thus, Main Street was born. But it couldn't have been in a worse spot.

The west side of the town was beautifully situated, with magnificent oak openings and good, firm ground. By contrast, the east side, where most of the town was situated, was swampy and in many spots impassable in bad weather. To illustrate this point, it should be noted that in 1844, a wagon remained stuck upright in a sinkhole located at the intersection of Main and Second Streets. Nevertheless, the advantage of the east side over the west side was in the fact that on the west side there was no clear title to land holdings, whereas there was no question of ownership of land on the east side of the city. Thus, eastern Watertown rose to greater prominence over western Watertown.

JOHN W. COLE'S FEED STORE. This 1866 image shows Cole's second store, opened across the street from the very first store in Watertown. This is how that first store, which was opened in 1841 by the Cole brothers, might have looked. (Watertown Historical Society collection.)

WATERTOWN IN 1842. This painting, done from the recollections of Eliza Cole in the 1890s by renowned artist Hubert Conner, shows what the settlement may have looked like at the time.

With the establishment of the first hotel and store and the creation of Main Street, things began to happen in Watertown, starting in 1842 with the granting of township status, which was soon followed by an official plat of the city that laid it out in lots and blocks in 1844. Milo Jones of nearby Fort Atkinson conducted this survey. Previously, the city had been crudely laid out in sections by two different individuals: Charles H. Goodhue who laid out the east side, and Patrick Rogan who laid out the west side.

This was followed by the erection of the first bridge across the Rock River at Main Street. This bridge was built in the winter of 1843 and paid for by public subscription. It was a bow-span bridge and lay quite close to the water. In fact, one had to go downhill to get on it and uphill to leave it.

As the decade progressed, new industries began to spring up. Patrick Rogan opened a second sawmill on the west side of the river in 1841 and another mill, called the Rough & Ready, was begun in 1847 on the far eastern portion of the river by Luther Cole and John Richards. Another mill, the Eclipse, was opened by Lyman Boomer on the far western portion of the river, but this enterprise did not last very long. Most industries were located along the Rock River at this time in order to take advantage of the waterpower to propel their machinery. Timothy

Johnson wrote his brother-in-law in 1845, "We have one of the greatest warter powers in the cuntry. Warter mashenry for three miles, as thick as they are amind to bild and warter anough to propell it."

John Richards is worthy of more than a passing reference. He was a former school teacher and one-time lawyer from Massachusetts. In the fall of 1836, he and a friend, John Chadwick, who later founded the brick industry in the city, set out on foot from their home state and walked to Watertown, arriving here in the spring of 1837. He purchased a parcel of land located along what is today known as East Gate Drive, on the eastern border of the city, and hung out his shingle as an attorney, becoming the first to do so in Jefferson County.

Richards's career continued to grow. In addition to farming, he owned the Rough & Ready Mill and also a lind-seed oil mill. His many investments would enable him to live the life of a gentleman. Despite his wealth, or perhaps in spite of it, he behaved in a very peculiar fashion. In the wintertime, for example, he would stuff straw into his boots and tie his coat with a rope belt. In truth, he looked like a tramp. But this "tramp" was in actuality one of the wealthiest men in the city. He even rose to the office of mayor of the city in the 1860s.

He is chiefly remembered today for having built an unusual private home for his family. In 1854, he finished work on an eight-sided brick mansion built on

THE ROUGH & READY MILL. Built in 1847 by Heber Smith, Luther Cole, and John Richards, this mill stood on South Concord Avenue until it burned to the ground in 1888.

THE OCTAGON HOUSE, c. 1870. Pictured in front of this eight-sided landmark are its original builder and owners, John and Eliza (Forbes) Richards. John Richards was the first attorney in Jefferson County and a prominent mill owner and gentleman farmer. He died in 1874, followed by his wife in 1902. (Gerald Kreitzman collection.)

a hilltop in the southeastern part of the city. His home boasted five-stories and included rudimentary forms of warm running water, central air-conditioning, and central heating. After the death of the last descendant residing in the home, the remaining family members gave the house to the newly formed Watertown Historical Society in 1937. Today, the Octagon House, as it is known, is operated as Watertown's public museum.

Milling was not the only industry to gain a foothold here at this time. The 1840s was a time of great improvements and new businesses were establishing themselves right and left. During this decade, a woolen mill opened on what is now South Water Street, as well as an iron foundry, wagon factories, furniture factories, and breweries. Cottage industries such as shoemaking, tailoring, millinery shops, and the like also thrived, especially with the arrival of immigrants to the area.

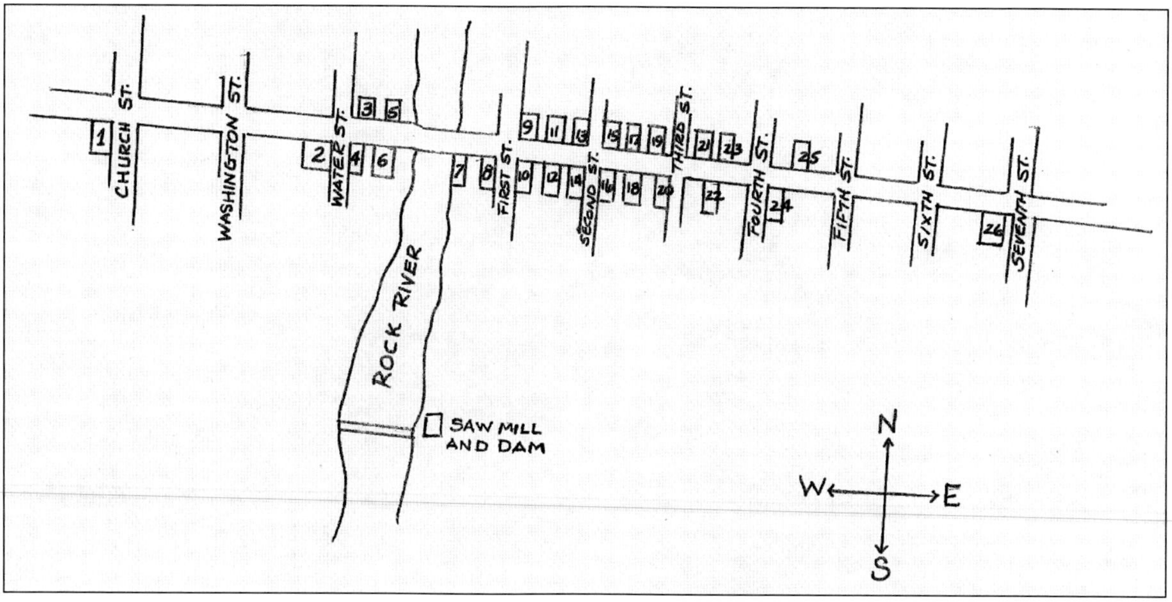

Main Street in 1845. There were only 26 buildings on the street at this time: 1. St. Bernard's Catholic Church, 2. American House Hotel, 3. Francis O'Rourke's grocery, 4. James Rogan's shanty, 5. Thomas Raidt's store, 6. Dr. Edward Johnson's drug store, 7. Linus R. Cady's law office, 8. a shanty, 9. The Exchange Hotel, 10. Planters Hotel, 11. Stimpson & Waldron's store, 12. William Besley's store, 13. John W. Cole's feed store, 14. William Ament's store, 15. The German Store, 16. Gust Cady's store, 17. a shanty, 18. Granger's house, 19. Stephen March's cabinet shop, 20. Mr. Duffy's house, 21. Perry's cooper shop, 22. a frame building, 23. William Besley's house, 24. Mr. Stimpson's house, 25. Mr. Cushman's house, and 26. an old house.

Homes began to spring up, and in 1845, Timothy Johnson could write to his brother-in-law with a sense of awe that:

> Our cuntry is a settling beyond all conseption. We have a little village in Watertown, five stoars, 2 taverns, 3 groseries, one apothecary shop, eight blacksmiths, one furnic, two saw mills, one grist mill, two meeting houses, schools, etc. The number of dwelling houses I cannot tell for they are putting up fore or five a day sum days. We shall have the largest town in the territory except Milwaukee.

Indeed, by 1846, the population of Watertown had increased from 200 in 1840 to an amazing 2,362 people. By 1846, the town contained six dry-goods stores, a grist or flouring mill, two sawmills, one woolen factory, one iron foundry, one brewery, one fanning mill factory, one hardware store, one drug store, four grocery stores, one rake factory, two cooper or barrel-making shops, one wagonmaker's shop, four tailor shops, four shoemaker shops, one milliner, four blacksmith shops, one bakery, one meat market, and one saddle and harness maker. Main Street at this time contained a little over 25 buildings, though not one was made of brick. The street itself was very low and filled with ruts and tree stumps. It was just wide enough for two teams to pass each other.

Until 1843 or so, most of the inhabitants of Watertown were either Yankees or Irish. In 1843, with unrest in Europe, Watertown began to experience its first major influx of the ethnic group that would forever be identified with the city: the Germans.

A few Germans had found their way here as early as 1837, but in no significant number. The 1843 arrivals came in large groups. Many settled in the nearby town of Lebanon, located to the north of the city. These were a class of Germans referred to as "The Old Lutherans," who had left Germany to avoid being forced to worship in the state-run United Evangelical Church. They were farmers for the most part, but a few of their numbers found city life more to their liking and chose to settle in Watertown.

CATTLE FAIR OR "VIEHMARKET," JUNE 1866. This monthly produce market was founded by German settlers in 1860 and is one of the oldest market days in Wisconsin. (Watertown Historical Society collection.)

THE BOHEMIAN SECTION OF WATERTOWN. This c. 1875 image depicts the area along South Concord and Oconomowoc Avenues where new arrivals from Bohemia (today's Slovakia and the Czech Republic) preferred to settle. (Watertown Historical Society collection.)

The Germans who followed these 1843 settlers came from all classes and began to open shops and establish social clubs. They brought with them a heritage and culture that was not seen here before. Among the traditions the German settlers established in Watertown were singing societies, the first one being founded in 1847, and perhaps the longest-lasting tradition, the monthly "Viehmarkt" or cattle fair, which has been held in the city since October 1860. Originally intended for farmers to come together to sell cattle and produce, today "Fair Day" is mainly devoted to the selling of plants, farm produce, and small items. Animals are no longer a part of the monthly event. Fred L. Holmes, in his 1944 book *Old World Wisconsin*, wrote wistfully of Watertown's monthly cattle fair, saying, "I am glad that I saw all this. The memory of these distinguished habits of country life, that are slowly passing, hangs in my mind like a lovely old picture."

German settlers increased from day to day, encouraged by their fellow countrymen. Most of these new arrivals brought money with them with which to buy property. One early American settler in Watertown remarked, "If it were not for the Germans with the capital and their industriousness, it would have been impossible for us Americans to hold our own."

With the revolution and unrest in Germany in 1848, Watertown began to see an increasing tide of a new class of German arrivals, the displaced intellectual. These Germans were often sarcastically referred to as "Latin Farmers," for it was said that most knew more about the dead languages than they did about the practical side of pioneer life in the new world. Nevertheless, it was this very class that spawned such important figures as Carl Schurz and gave Watertown its unique character.

German is no longer heard on Watertown's streets as it once was, but the heritage is still there in the names of families and in other ways. In his book *Old World Wisconsin*, Fred Holmes quotes a local farmer who said, "Maybe in another 100 years people in this section will no longer speak German, but the customs will never die. They belong to the race."

Immigration to Watertown and the vicinity from the mid-1840s was almost exclusively German. Once here, Germans tended to settle on the east side of the river and also in the northern parts of the city. The Irish, by comparison, tended to settle on the west side of the river and in the southern parts of the city. The Yankees and other ethnic groups took what was left. The other dominant ethnic groups in Watertown were Bohemians and Welsh. The Bohemians, who would

ST. BERNARD'S CATHOLIC CHURCH. This c. 1860 image shows the original church edifice, which was removed in 1876 when the present brick church was built. This was the first Catholic church in Watertown.

begin arriving in the late 1840s and 1850s, settled in the southeastern part of the city, and the Welsh, who began to immigrate to this area in the 1840s, settled on farms located on the western edge of Watertown. Thus, by the 1850s and 1860s, Watertown was a city of "settlements." Each ethnic area was a little entity unto itself, often complete with stores and saloons. These settlements would physically last until the turn of the century and even today, parts of the city are still identified with certain ethnic groups.

The influx of immigrants led to tensions, most notably between the Germans and the Irish. Often the two groups would come to blows. Public gatherings or dances were often marred by ugly altercations. The English-speaking settlers ran local government and tried, unsuccessfully, to keep the foreign element out. As the number of Germans rose, the Irish soon began to be outnumbered and, little by little, Germans began to make political inroads. A satirical poem from the mid-1800s makes pointed references to the inequity of the ruling class in Watertown:

ST. HENRY'S CATHOLIC CHURCH. Founded in 1853, this was the German Catholic church. A separate house of worship was needed since there were bad relations between the Germans and the Irish in Watertown at that time. (Watertown Historical Society collection.)

JOHN CHADWICK. Chadwick founded the brick industry in Watertown in 1847. (Watertown Historical Society collection.)

Oh Wasserstadt, oh Wasserstadt, was ist bei dir passiert?
Dass in dein schoenes, Deutsches Stadt
Das Irisch Volk regiert!
(Oh Watertown, Oh Watertown, what 'ere did you befall?
That in your lovely German city
The Irish rule you all!)

The separation of Irish and Germans even extended to religion. In Watertown, the only Catholic church was Saint Bernard's, which was established by the Reverend Martin Kundig in 1841 and was the house of worship for the Irish of the area. German Catholics had to make do on their own until 1853 when Saint Henry's Catholic Church opened. This was a German Catholic church located on the east side of the river. However, it is interesting to note that the first traveling priest to say Mass in Watertown was a German.

The 1840s marked the creation of most of the churches in the city. At least six different churches were established during this time period. Of these, Saint Bernard's Catholic Church, established in 1843; the First Congregational Church, established in 1845; Saint Paul's Episcopal Church, established in 1845; and Saint Luke's Lutheran Church, established in 1849, are still in existence. They joined the Methodist church, which had been established in Watertown in 1837.

A WATERTOWN BRICKYARD IN THE LATE 1890S. Bricks were manufactured in Watertown from 1847 to the early 1930s. (Watertown Historical Society collection.)

The 1840s also saw a movement afoot to establish a public school system. The first steps were taken in 1844 with the founding of the first school board. At this time, churches either ran most schools in the city or there were private institutions run by so-called professors. The newly formed school board met to establish a public system. At the first meeting, it was voted that two-thirds of the public monies were to be used for the winter school term and one-third for the summer session. At a later meeting, a resolution was passed to raise $30 for the purpose of hiring a schoolroom for the winter. Money was still scarce at this time, so the school board trustees were empowered to sell the stove and pipe to raise the necessary amount. One wonders how students could be expected to concentrate in the wintertime with no stove to heat the room! A properly uniform school system would not be established in Watertown until the 1850s.

By 1847, the citizens of Watertown were agitating for better transportation routes. A stage line ran through the city as early as 1844, but travel was still difficult. The idea of building a network of wooden highways was proposed and, accordingly, a gala ball was held in Watertown to raise awareness of their importance and also to raise the necessary start-up costs. Though not completed until 1853, the Watertown Plank Road would prove to be very successful and provide yet another compelling reason to bring people to Watertown.

By the end of the decade, wooden homes in Watertown were giving way to magnificent brick structures as the first brickyards began to open. John Chadwick and his brother David were the first to manufacture bricks here, and their brickyard would soon spawn others until at least six brickyards were in operation by the 1850s. A total of ten million bricks were being produced annually in Watertown by the 1860s.

Watertown brick was very much like Cream City bricks made in Milwaukee. They were a golden tan in color for the most part and quite porous. Watertown bricks were first used to build a house in 1847 when the home of Pliny D. Bassford was constructed. The first brick hotel soon followed. The *Watertown Chronicle* on January 19, 1848 remarked, "It will be a few years before the wonder is, not that brick dwellings are erected, but that wood is used at all."

The brick industry slowly began to dwindle by the end of the nineteenth century and, by the early days of the twentieth century, there were only two brickyards still in business. That number would shrink to one before the industry ceased to exist in Watertown in the early 1930s.

BRICK HOUSE. This house is believed to be the first in Watertown to be constructed entirely of brick. (Watertown Historical Society collection.)

JONATHAN A. HADLEY. Hadley was the founder of the first newspaper in Watertown, the Watertown Chronicle, *which made its appearance on June 23, 1847. (Watertown Historical Society collection.)*

In 1847, Watertown left its pioneer days behind when the first weekly newspaper began operations. The *Watertown Chronicle* made its appearance on June 23, 1847. The editor and publisher of the paper was Jonathan A. Hadley, a native of New Hampshire. He would run his paper until 1853 when he left to make a run at politics, serving for a time as state assessor. Hadley's newspaper would last until 1856.

Shortly after the *Chronicle* made its grand entrance, a second newspaper began to appear, the *Rock River Pilot*, founded by George Hyer. This paper had a very short run, coming to a close in 1848. Other papers would follow throughout the 1850s on through the 1930s, making a total of 22 different newspapers to be published in Watertown.

The first German-run brewery was opened in November 1847 by Johann Jacob Hoeffner, a native of the Rhineland. His brewery, which was built of brick and called the Red Brick Brewery, produced eight to ten barrels of beer a week. It was consumed with great relish by the thirsty citizens of Watertown. The Red Brick Brewery quickly out-classed the first brewery to open here, an ale brewery founded by William Anson in 1846, which produced a decidedly inferior product. According to one history, half the town was made sick from the consumption of Anson's ale. Brewing would become a major industry, reaching its peak in the 1860s, but by the 1880s, it was in decline. By 1900, only one brewery would still exist in the city, the Hartig Company, which lasted until 1947.

The decade ended with Watertown being granted a village charter in 1849 by the state legislature. The decade had witnessed a dramatic rise in the population of the village from a little over 200 in 1840 to over 3,000 by 1850. But for all of that, Watertown still had a long way to go. C.C. Hamlin, an early settler, left an evocative word picture of the city at this time when he wrote the following:

THE RED BRICK BREWERY. Founded by Johann Jacob Hoeffner in 1847, this was the first lager brewery in town and would be the start of the brewing industry in Watertown.

> Streets with high sounding names, but filled with staves and stones and stumps, timber and tamarack poles, and saw logs; emigrant wagons and other kinds of vehicles, rough, uncouth-looking men, unkempt boys; Indians almost in a state of nudity, with here and there a woman hurrying by; but the greatest curiosity was the German emigrants, without any knowledge of our language, but with wistful eyes peering into one's face, as if to find friends far away from their native land . . . A town of "sheboygans" or slab shanties, with here and there a decent looking dwelling house; a medley of all things imaginable, chaos come again, it seemed.

Good times were on the horizon. The pioneer days in Watertown had ended. A boom in building and in business was about to erupt, the likes of which Watertown had never seen before. The local newspaper, the *Watertown Chronicle*, reported on January 19, 1848 that, "Those who appreciate the immense capabilities of the surrounding country, and its admirable location on a never failing river, have termed Watertown the future Rochester of the west."

NEUMANN & KRUEGER CIGAR FACTORY. This c. 1900 image shows one of the many cigar factories that flourished in Watertown from the 1850s through the 1940s.

4. Boom Town Days: 1850–1860

Watertown holds out rare inducements to immigrant businessmen and mechanics. Its inexhaustible water power, the fertility of the surrounding country, and the abundance of timber in its immediate vicinity, give the town advantages possessed by no other in all the west. Add to this that its remoteness from Milwaukee, though connected therewith by a plank road, relieves it of all legitimate business competition with that city, and business men and mechanics designing to settle in this state, cannot well fail of seeing at once that Watertown presents advantages which it would not be wisdom in them to overlook.

Watertown Chronicle, April 23, 1851

The 1850s were a time of unprecedented growth for Watertown. Houses were being built, new industries began, and the tide of foreign immigrants, mainly Germans, continued to steadily grow. This boom was due in large part to two things: the opening of the Watertown Plank Road and the arrival of the railroad shortly thereafter.

The plank road had been under construction for several years. It was, as its name would imply, a road or highway made of wooden planks. The construction of the highway was a slow process, made more difficult by having to push the road over rough, uneven terrain and through periods of bad weather. It was completed to Watertown in June 1853. It roughly followed what is today State Highway 16 and entered the city along East Gate Drive. The Watertown Plank Road was a toll road and there were two toll gates located in Watertown. One was at the eastern end of East Gate Drive and the other near the intersection of West Main Street and Dayton Street on the west side of the city. The last remaining tollhouse was torn down in 1999.

For a few years, the plank road proved to be a godsend. It decreased the normal travel time between Milwaukee and Watertown from six days to three days, and allowed heavy loads to be transported with ease.

But the handwriting was on the wall and once the first train arrived, the plank road soon became superfluous. It reverted to state ownership by the 1880s and ceased to be operated as a toll road. It was abandoned and left to rot and ruin. By the early days of the twentieth century, the plank road was merely a memory.

EAST GATE TOLL HOUSE, WATERTOWN PLANK ROAD. There were two toll houses in Watertown at one time, this one and another near the intersection of West Main and Dayton Streets. This one was torn down in the late 1990s. (Watertown Historical Society collection.)

It was the railroad that made the most headlines during this time period. The city fathers were very anxious to have the "iron horse" come through the city and actively campaigned to have the line directed through Watertown. It should have been an almost foregone conclusion that Watertown would get a rail line, since the city was in the favored position of being almost dead center between Milwaukee, the largest city in the state, and Madison, Wisconsin's capital. Still, the city fathers were not taking any chances and, accordingly, they began to offer a series of financial inducements, beginning in 1853, to the newly formed Milwaukee & Watertown Railway.

In March 1853, an act of the state legislature enabled the city to lend its credit to the Milwaukee & Watertown Railway. On August 1, 1853, the city delivered to the directors of the road an $80,000 loan to run 10 years at 8 percent interest. In turn, the railroad company was to deliver to the city a bond and execute a mortgage on their road for a sum of $80,000 once the line was completed as far as the city of Oconomowoc, located to the east of Watertown.

In 1855, the legislature authorized the city to issue bonds to aid the Watertown & Madison Railway to the amount of $50,000 and it also enabled the city to give an additional $40,000 to the Milwaukee & Watertown Railway. In 1856, the state legislature allowed the city to issue $400,000 worth of bonds, half of which was to aid the Watertown & Madison Railway and the other half for the Chicago, St. Paul & Fond du Lac Railway. Also in 1856, the Watertown & Madison and Milwaukee & Watertown Railways were consolidated, and this new consolidation would later become the Milwaukee Road.

This issuance of bonds continued with the support of the city and the state legislature through 1857. By this time, the Watertown & Madison Railway had received $1,050,000 in bonds and mortgages. Watertown had issued $100,000, $185,000 was in farm mortgages, and the railroad itself issued $10,000 in first mortgage bonds for every mile of road. Citizens in the various towns along the line also bought shares of stock.

The legislature of 1857 authorized the Watertown & Madison Railway to extend its line to the Mississippi River. Legislators from Watertown were given a testimonial dinner in honor of their efforts in promoting the extension of the road. Everyone had dreams of getting rich because of the railroad. D.W. Ballou, editor of the *Watertown Democrat*, recalled, "Those were exciting and lively times, when all were full of boundless confidence that the reality would be what the fancy painted it, without a thought of the rough breakers ahead."

Business people, in preparation for the impending arrival of the railroad, began to build huge brick blocks of stores. The *Watertown Democrat* in its issue of May 22, 1856, commented on this fact by stating the following:

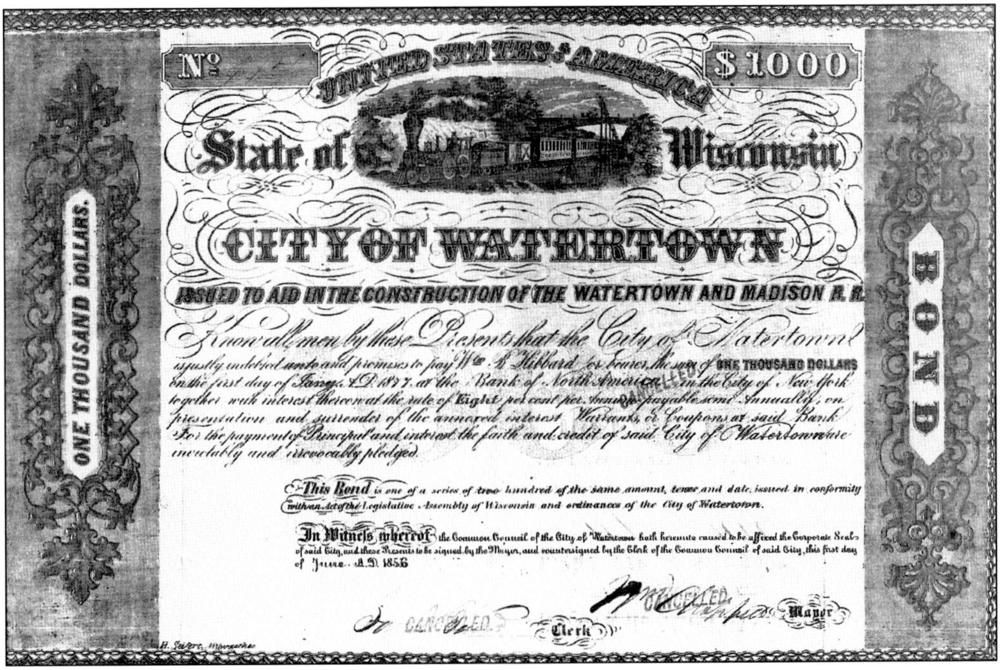

A WATERTOWN RAILROAD BOND. *Bonds like this one for $1,000 helped raise money to build the Watertown & Madison Railway. (Watertown Historical Society collection.)*

MAIN STREET, C. 1855. This is how Main Street in Watertown looked the year the railroad came through the city.

> The steady increase of business has made these additional buildings a necessity. For years past the demand for stores has been greater than the supply, and everything indicates this will continue to be so for a long time to come. This is owing to the fact that our city is growing in numbers and the country around it in all directions [is] improving in value . . . Every day does something for us in the way of improvement, population and wealth.

The very character and look of Watertown's Main Street was created during this time.

Stores catering to every possible group and want opened. It is amusing to note that at this time there was a Yankee Store, an American Store, and a Dutch Store located on Main Street. Many stores, hoping to entice the emigrant trade, announced that German-speaking clerks were on hand to assist foreigners.

Banking began at this time with the founding of the first bank in Watertown, called the Jefferson County Bank, by Daniel Jones in 1853. Jones was a native of New Hampshire who had come to Watertown in 1845 and opened a store. He branched out into financial services in 1852. The Jefferson County Bank was short-lived, however, and it suspended business in 1862. Jones then joined forces with a new concern, the Wisconsin National Bank, which was founded in 1858. The Wisconsin National Bank later became the Valley Bank and, in 1994, this firm was taken over by the M&I Bank Corporation.

Another pioneer bank was the Bank of Watertown, founded in 1854 by A.L. Pritchard, who lived in New York. The longtime cashier of this bank was William H. Clark who was sent to Watertown by Pritchard to run the concern. In the 1960s, this bank became a branch of the Marshall and Ilsley Corporation.

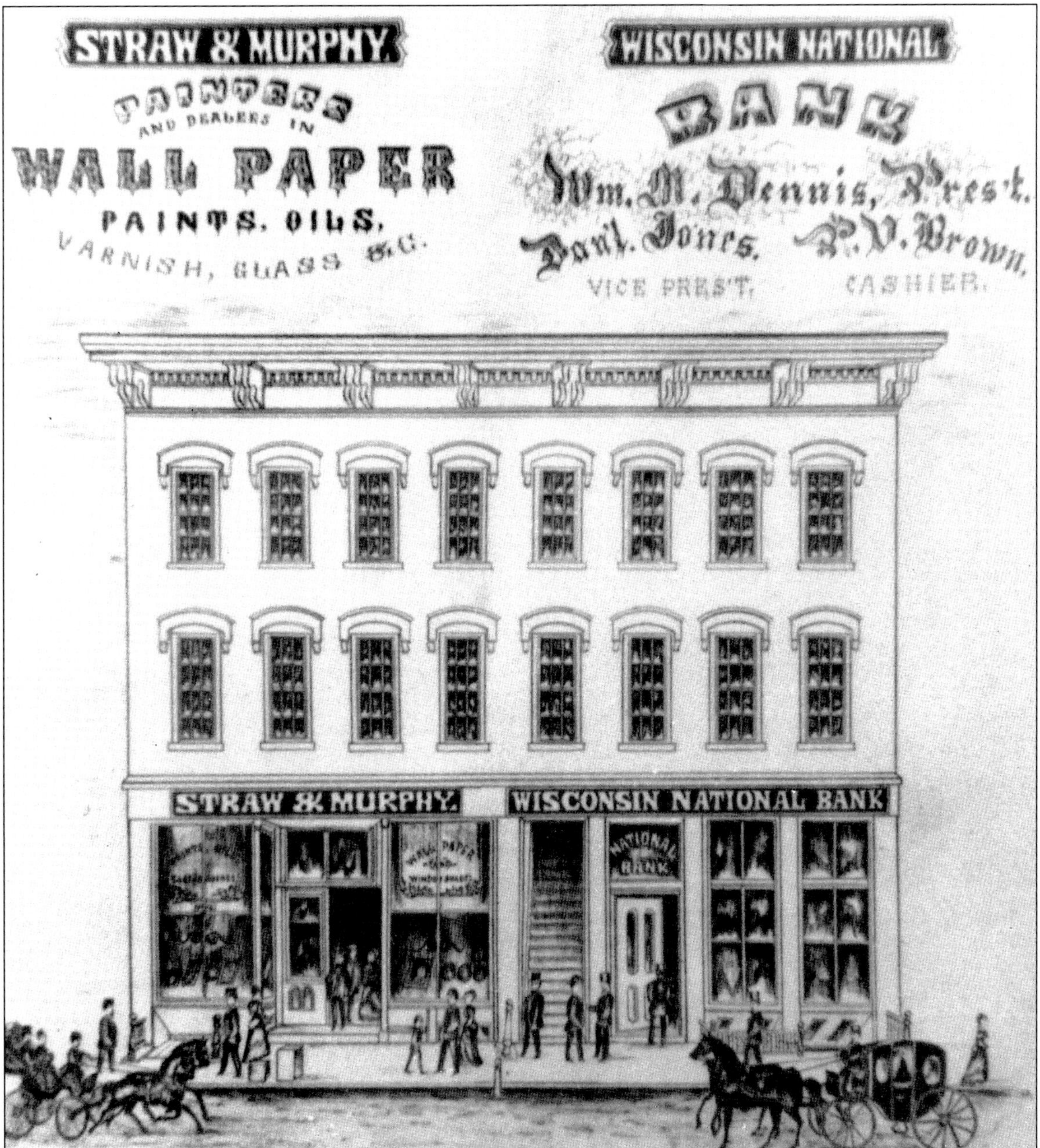

THE WISCONSIN NATIONAL BANK. The first bank in Watertown had been founded in 1854 by Daniel Jones. The Wisconsin National Bank was the third bank to be started in Watertown. (Watertown Historical Society collection.)

WILLIAM C. CHAPPELL. Chappell was mayor of Watertown in 1856 and was one of the city's most bombastic government officials. He hired thugs to blast a cannon in the business district in order to destroy the windows of a political foe. (Watertown Historical Society collection.)

There were two other banks founded in the city, the Merchants Bank, founded in 1892 and now known as Bank One, and the Farmers and Citizens Bank, founded in 1912. The latter ceased operations in 1956. In 1920, a further financial institution, the Watertown Building and Loan, was organized. It still operates today as the Associated Bank.

A Watertown booster book written by E.B. Quiner in 1856 gave a statistical listing of the city's retail and commercial enterprises and stated that, at this time, Watertown had the following: 9 churches, 12 schools and academies, 28 dry good stores, 24 grocery stores, 5 hardware stores, 4 drugstores, 6 clothing stores, 1 crockery store, 6 boot and shoe stores, 3 fancy toy stores, 2 leather stores, 2 banks, 10 hotels, 5 livery stables, 5 tin shops, 1 copper shop, 5 cabinet warehouses, 4 millinery shops, 3 bookstores, 3 printing offices, 1 foundry, 5 meat markets, 5 double saw mills, 2 flouring mills, 1 oil mill, 1 woolen factory, 1 hoe and fork factory, 2 door and blind factories, 1 soap factory, 1 tobacconist shop, 3 paint shops, 14 carriage shops, 29 blacksmith shops, 9 cooper shops, 2 gunsmiths, 1 manufacturing confectioner, 1 locksmith, 2 barber shops, 4 harness shops, 1 machine shop, 2 turning shops, 2 planing mills, 5 carpenter shops, 5 plow shops, 1 furnace, 3 jewelry stores, 1 Dauguerran gallery, 2 dentists, 5 bakeries, 7 lumber yards, 6 brick yards, 1 ashery, 15 warehouses, 1 gas works, 4 insurance agencies, 1 portrait painter, 3 breweries, 1 Sons of Temperance, and 1 Odd Fellows. (This last obviously refers to a club and not, as it is supposed, to the citizenry.)

But it was not just commercial improvements. Homes were being erected at an alarming rate. One newspaper reported that the sound of hammering and sawing was non-stop and that whole buildings were going up seemingly over night. Brick was the material of choice. Not only did brick have a feeling of permanence, but also it had one added advantage: it was harder to burn. This was very fortunate for the city, since there was no fire department in Watertown until 1857.

Everything was growing beyond all proportion. Large landholders, such as John W. Cole and William M. Dennis (both of whom would serve as mayors), began to cash in on their property by subdividing their land into lots and selling them off. These later became additions to the city. The practice was so prevalent that an 1850 census recap published in the *Democratic State Register*, one of the local newspapers in Watertown at the time, reported population returns not only from the city, but also from "Dennisville and Colesburg."

Carl Schurz. Schurz was a political refugee of the Revolution in Germany of 1848. He settled for a short time in Watertown before moving on to bigger and better things. (John Reichardt collection.)

Watertown was granted a city charter in March 1853 and in due course, the first mayor was elected. This was Theodore Prentice, a native of Vermont. The first mayors were Yankees. It would be some time before the first German would be elected mayor. With the beginnings of a mayor-alderman system, Watertown would be treated to a stream of government leaders that ranged from the sublime to the ridiculous. The latter category would have to include Joseph Lindon, a former meat-packer, hotel keeper, and horse thief, and William Chappell, whose vitriolic temperament would lead him to hire thugs to blast a cannon in the commercial section of the city, destroying plate-glass windows on several buildings.

MARGARETHE MEYER SCHURZ. Mrs. Schurz founded the first kindergarten in America in a small building in Watertown. The building is now a national shrine.

PIONEER ENGINE COMPANY. This photograph shows the interior of the first fire department in Watertown, founded in 1857. (Watertown Historical Society collection.)

Germans began to make inroads in local politics beginning in the 1850s with the election of, among others, Carl Schurz as an alderman for the Fifth Ward of the city. Schurz (1809–1906), who is known today as a German-American patriot, had come to Watertown in 1855. His uncle Jacob Juessen was living here and having family in the city convinced him that this would be a perfect place to settle. He brought his wife, Margarethe, to Watertown and built her a lovely home in the northern part of the city. He wrote to his wife in glowing terms about their new home in 1855: "You can scarcely believe how rapidly this town is growing. Since I was here last, whole rows of three-story buildings have been built. Very soon the main street will have lost its character of a country town."

Schurz became a notary in the city and also owned and edited a short-lived newspaper, *Der Volkzeitung* (*The People's Paper*). He made his first political speech in the city of Jefferson, the county seat, and this whetted his appetite for a life in politics. He moved his family to Milwaukee in the latter 1850s and, from there, embarked on a political career that would lead him ultimately to serve under several presidents, from Abraham Lincoln to Rutherford B. Hayes.

But in Watertown it is not Carl Schurz who is remembered and revered, for he was bitterly disliked by many in the city because he was, among other things, an ardent Republican. No, it is his wife, Margarethe, who is honored for her founding of the first kindergarten in the United States in 1856. This preschool for children was a revolutionary idea at the time and later adopted by other educators. The building that once housed Mrs. Schurz's kindergarten is today a public museum in Watertown.

JOHN D. "PUT" REICHARDT. "Put," a former bareback circus rider in Germany, was one of Watertown's earliest and most celebrated police constables. (John Reichardt collection.)

With the granting of a city charter, Watertown began to flex its muscles and a number of civic improvements were started, such as the establishment of a fire department and police force. Watertown had a bucket brigade as early as 1847, but had no real organized fire fighting force until 1857 when a group of citizens, led by Carl Schurz, petitioned the city fathers to purchase the necessary equipment to fight fires. Accordingly, a "water witch," or pumping engine, was purchased and suitable lengths of hosepipe and buckets were procured. However, the early firemen were a rag-tag lot and no real organization came about until much later.

As for a police force, until the turn of the century, Watertown had to make do with local constables, justices of the peace for each ward, and a night watch. Proper police methods were not put into force until the arrival in office of Herman C. Block, who can be considered the founder of the Watertown Police Department as it is known today. Still, the early law-keepers were a hardy lot.

Notable constables included John "Put" Reichert, a former bareback rider with a circus in Germany. A formidable man, he would sneak up behind suspected law-breakers and slap his truncheon on the ground shouting, "Put, boys, put!" The offenders would then scatter in all directions.

Another lawman worthy of note was Joseph Giles, who rose to the rank of sheriff. He was a former clerk in a general store in Watertown and acted as an interpreter for Ho-Chunk Native Americans. Giles was a man of dogged resolve. He was once chasing a criminal through the city and the offender ran to the banks of the Rock River. Faced with the prospect of Giles on his trail and the river before him, he chose to jump into the river and swim to safety. Giles was described as having a long, flowing white beard that would have made him look very distinguished except for his habit of chewing tobacco, which left a long streak of brown residue down the center of his hirsute glory.

Other civic improvements at this time included a standardized school system, which was established in 1856. This Union School System brought each of the satellite schools in Watertown in line with a common lesson plan. Thus, the first school district was born. In 1856, there were 426 students enrolled in the union schools in Watertown, though the city would still boast a number of private schools through the end of the nineteenth century.

UNION SCHOOL #2. Located in the upper right of this 1873 photograph, the school was erected in the late 1850s. It was torn down and rebuilt in 1909, when it became known as Lincoln School. This was part of the unified school system established in the mid-1850s in Watertown. (Watertown Historical Society collection.)

Sewer and gas were the final city improvements brought about in the 1850s. The sewer system was created in 1855 as a probable answer to the horrific cholera epidemic, which plagued the city each year from 1849 to 1854. Poor sanitation was the cause of the disease. The city fathers decided to clean up the city and install a system of brick-lined sewers in various sections. Full sewer and water hook-ups would not come until much later.

The Watertown City Gas Company began manufacturing gas at a plant in North Second Street in 1856. The presence of gas light on the streets and in homes was a great improvement and added to the safety of its citizens. The streets of the city were lit for the first time in July 1856. The *Watertown Democrat* reported the following on July 24th:

> Our streets, for the first time were lighted with gas last Monday night. The lampposts are high, and the burners shone brilliantly, throwing around a wide circle of light. This will be a great improvement wherever it is introduced. Main, West Avenue, Second, Fourth, Clyman and Washington are the streets along which lamps will be placed for the present. As soon as service pipes are put down along other streets, posts will be put up and lamps used.

WATERTOWN GAS WORKS. This 1925 image shows the gas works plant located on South Second and Clyman Streets. The gas company was founded in 1856.

KRUMENAUER POLLING PLACE. This was the site of illegal voting activity during the great "county seat war," which raged between Jefferson and Watertown in 1856. (Watertown Historical Society collection.)

Despite its initial success, however, the gas plant closed in 1864 due to lack of patronage. A group of citizens saved the company and ultimately it proved to be successful. By 1903, there were almost 900 customers served by the gas company. In 1905, the Watertown Gas and Electric Company purchased the Watertown Gas Company and later it became a part of the Wisconsin Gas and Electric Company. In 1928, the gas-making plant closed and customers began to receive gas through pipelines from gas producing fields elsewhere.

In addition to internal improvements, Watertown began to flex its muscles in county matters. The village of Jefferson had originally been chosen as the county seat because of its central location. However, by the 1850s, Watertown had grown to be the largest city in the county, while Jefferson was still a small town. There arose a feeling among the citizens of Watertown at this time that perhaps the county seat should be transferred from Jefferson to Watertown.

In 1856, William Chappell, a member of the state legislature and mayor of Watertown, introduced a bill in the state assembly to let the voters decide whether Jefferson or Watertown should be the county seat. In order to ensure that Watertown would win this contest, Chappell also started litigation to authorize the annexation of five southern townships of Dodge County to Jefferson County on the pretext that Dodge County's land area exceeded its legal rights. This was contested by the county clerk of Dodge County on the grounds that Chappell's claim was unconstitutional. The issue came to a vote.

FRANKLIN COUNTY. This map shows the proposed new county, which would have had Watertown as its county seat.

It soon became clear that both sides were guilty of gross voting irregularities. The pro-Jefferson side made considerable use of the so-called Krumenauer polling place. This was a farm located in the middle of nowhere near Jefferson and it was the site of a supplemental voting point. Voters would, according to legend, first vote there using their own names and then reappear a few hours later and vote again using names pulled out of the Cincinnati City Directory. Nevertheless, despite these under-handed tricks, the vote showed that Watertown won by 4,518 to 2,545.

In desperation, the Jefferson side now came up with a compromise: they would allow a new county to be organized to be composed of five Dodge County townships and the towns of Watertown, Ixonia, and part of Milford. This county was to have been given the name Franklin, and Watertown would be its capital, but this plan did not meet with much favor and the state legislature completely shot it down. So, in January 1857, the county board met in Watertown as mandated by the election and it seemed very bleak for Jefferson's future. Later that year, however, the Wisconsin Supreme Court decided against Chappell and his annexation scheme, and it invalidated the votes of the Dodge County residents. Without those votes, Watertown lost the election and the county seat reverted once more to Jefferson where it has remained ever since.

New churches began to spring up to serve the needs of the newly arrived immigrants. The first Lutheran church, Saint John's, opened in 1852, followed by Saint Henry's, a German Catholic church, in 1853. The second Lutheran church to be established here was Saint Mark's in 1854 and the first Moravian Church began in 1853. The Moravians brought with them the practice of celebrating the New Year with the blowing of horns at midnight and the glorifying of Christmas through the use of decorative pieces around and beneath the Christmas tree, something that had never been seen in the city until then. Other churches founded in the nineteenth century in Watertown included the Advent Church, founded in 1873, the First Baptist Church (which transferred from nearby Lebanon, Wisconsin) in 1882, and Immanuel Lutheran Church, a splinter group made up of members of Saint Mark's in 1875. This last named church began when a minister from Saint Mark's, Pastor Heinrichs, was

EARLY MILWAUKEE ROAD LOCOMOTIVE. This c. 1860 photograph shows one of the first locomotives to come through Watertown. (Watertown Historical Society collection.)

discharged for drunkenness. Heinrichs had such a loyal following, however, that several members of the congregation followed their minister, whom they felt was wrongly discharged, and founded their own church. After wrangling with the Wisconsin Synod officers for a few years over its legal standing, the newly created Immanuel Lutheran Church was formally recognized. There are today, at last count, over 25 churches that minister to the spiritual needs of people living in Watertown.

But all of these innovations and improvements paled in comparison to the arrival of the railroad, which was the greatest event of the decade. When that first engine arrived in Watertown on September 21, 1855, Watertown's prominence was secured. Almost overnight, the city's population swelled to over 8,500 and, by 1856, that number had risen to nearly 10,000, making Watertown the second largest city in Wisconsin at that time.

As befitting its size and prominence, Watertown hosted the Wisconsin State Fair in 1853 and also began to boast of musical societies and pleasure spots. German residents founded the first singing society, known as "Der Liedertafel," in 1847. In the 1850s, this became the Watertown Musical Society. It merged with the newly formed Watertown Philharmonic Society in the early 1860s and became the Concordia Musical Society under the direction of organ-maker Emil C. Gaebler. This organization produced many operas and operettas featuring local talent and was Watertown's longest lasting musical association.

As for pleasure spots, Watertown has always had more than its fair share of saloons, but in the 1850s, a new form of the saloon opened, the Sommergarten. These were spots where one could have a drink under the canopy of trees, indulge in a little archery or shooting, enjoy a good meal and in the evenings, "trip the light fantastic." The first to open was a spot on West Main Street known as Der Freischuetz in 1853, near the western terminus of the plank road. This establishment proved to be very successful and by the end of the decade, there were several other spots in the city, such as Herrmann's Garten, Racek's Garten, and Cech's Garten. Der Freischuetz lasted till the 1880s, though by then it had slipped in quality and was known by its more common name, the Mud Tavern. It was torn down in the early 1920s.

Just when everything seemed to be going so well for Watertown, the bubble burst. A nationwide depression broke out in 1857 and it caused every railroad company in the state to fail. As these failed, everyone who had pinned their hopes on getting rich began to realize that they were ruined. Red auction flags began to be seen more and more on buildings along Main Street and the population of the city began to fall as quickly as it had grown. For a time, the people of Watertown were unaware of just how much of a calamitous situation they had gotten themselves into, but they would soon learn.

The end of the decade was marked with one further disastrous event, brought about, coincidentally, by the railroad. On November 3, 1859, a terrible accident occurred on the Chicago Northwestern Railway line 8 miles south of Watertown. The southbound passenger train ran over a large ox and was thrown from the track; five passenger cars were derailed and smashed to pieces. Eleven persons were killed, including Theron Minor, a former editor of the *Watertown Chronicle*, three were fatally injured, and twenty-five were badly hurt.

Thus, the 1850s and its good times came to an abrupt end and Watertown bravely lurched forward into a new decade, a little wiser, but totally unprepared for what was about to come: the Civil War.

THE MUD TAVERN. This was, reportedly, the very first German "Sommergarten," or pleasure spot, built in the city. It stood along West Main Street from 1853 until it was torn down in the early 1920s. The final owners, Mr. and Mrs. Carl Strege (the author's great-great-grandparents) are pictured in front of the tavern, c. 1900.

5. Watertown during the Civil War: 1860–1865

Last Saturday evening a public meeting was held at the headquarters of the volunteer company, for the purpose of raising a fund to provide for the families of those who enlist. Mayor Williams presided. The large and enthusiastic assemblage was eloquently addressed by Senator Gill, Hiram Barber, Carl Schurz and Emil Rothe. Committees were appointed for each ward, and we are informed that liberal subscriptions have already been made by many of our citizens. There is and will be but one sentiment here. Everybody is for maintaining the government. All who volunteer to fight the battles of our country will find a community willing to make their families comfortable, and pay whatever it may cost to prove that we "know our rights, and knowing dare maintain."

Watertown Democrat, April 25, 1861

One of the most momentous events of the nineteenth century was the Civil War, which raged with a fury between 1861 and 1865. Like most areas, Watertown was there from the start, sending forth its men and boys to do battle for the cause of the Union.

Actually, Watertown was never without some form of military fervor. As early as 1848, a recruiting office was opened in the city for the purpose of rounding up men to fight in the Mexican War. With the arrival of German immigrants, a military company was organized in 1853 that called itself the Watertown Rifles. This company drilled regularly, took part in patriotic displays on July 4th and Washington's Birthday, and even had its own uniforms. (The uniforms were lost along with their arms when the Western Star Hotel on Cady Street, where they had their headquarters, burned to the ground in 1860.) At the outbreak of the Civil War, this group disbanded, but its name was carried on by one of the first volunteer companies to be organized in the city in 1861.

Even before the Mexican War, Watertown had a small role in another military action, the Black Hawk War of 1832. In July 1832, Black Hawk, a Sauk chief, and his band came through the eastern part of Watertown while being pursued by General Henry Atkinson and his troops. Black Hawk and his followers hid out in the area around Hustisford. Then, when their camp was detected by the

THE WATERTOWN RIFLE COMPANY. This German artillery company was organized in 1853 and disbanded in 1861. (Watertown Historical Society collection.)

United States troops, the Native Americans raced towards the Four Lakes area around Madison and, in doing so, they crossed the Rock River about where the Main Street bridge is in downtown Watertown today. Among the participants in the Black Hawk War were Abraham Lincoln and Jefferson Davis, who, in 1839, bunked with James Rogan while leading a detachment of troops through the area. Both of these men later played important roles in the Civil War, Lincoln as president of the United States and Davis as president of the Confederacy.

Watertown was a strong Democratic city and so when Abraham Lincoln ran for president, his candidacy was met with strong opposition. The newly organized Republican Party, or "Wide-Awakes" as they called themselves, had a hard time convincing the German settlers in the city to vote for Lincoln. Through the efforts of Carl Schurz and his fiery orations, many who would have voted for Stephen A. Douglas were swayed to vote for Lincoln instead. But it wasn't all smooth sailing. In October 1860, Watertown was the scene of an ugly riot between Republicans for Lincoln and Democrats for Douglas.

It seems that the Republicans had planned a mass meeting in the city and they invited many supporters from surrounding areas to come there. Upon their arrival, they would stage a grand parade and hold a political rally. The Democrats, most of who were egged on by Emil Rothe, a refugee of the revolution of 1848, an agitator, and rabble-rouser, got wind of this and they decided to squelch the affair. The Republicans from out of town were met at the northwestern depot by an unruly mob that taunted and jeered at them. As they made their way through the crowd, brickbats and stones were hurled at them. The Republicans kept their composure, however, which only infuriated the mob even more. As the Republicans paraded down Main Street, they were confronted by a series of bonfires meant to halt their procession. The Wide-Awakes merely stepped around them. Even more enraged, the mob then resorted to grabbing burning sticks and throwing them at the marchers' feet. Some of the crowd began to throw cordwood at the marchers as well.

EMIL ROTHE. This editor of the local German-language newspaper and sometimes lawyer was one of the instigators of the so-called Republican Riot of 1860 that took place in Watertown. (Watertown Historical Society collection.)

But the crowning insult occurred after the rally ended. All during the speeches, the speakers were drowned out by the incessant catcalls of the anti-Lincoln mob. Lincoln banners were destroyed and Douglas banners were hung in front of the Republicans. After the rally, the Republicans commenced another march through the city and as they went by a saloon, the contents of a chamber pot were emptied on them. This was the last straw and the Republicans proceeded to rush into the saloon and beat the daylights out of the men inside. Thus ended the Republican riot.

A Democratic rally was scheduled to be held in Watertown the next week and the editor of the *Watertown Republican,* Justus Moak, cautioned his Republican brethren not to resort to the tactics of the Democrats. He wrote the following:

> If 4 or 5 hundred "little giants" . . . should be there, don't whack any of them over the heads with clubs. Don't throw stones and rotten eggs at them as they pass through the streets. Don't call them "a lot of god damned fools." Don't string a Lincoln flag across the street that they are to travel, as an insult. Don't get a crowd of boys together and tell them if they will "prevent the procession from passing you will give them all the beer they can drink." In a word, don't do anything that the Democrats did at our meeting last week, but . . . be civil and decent.

Lincoln was elected in 1860, despite all the protests and riots. Shortly after his election, Southern states began to secede from the Union and, on April 18, 1861, Fort Sumter was fired upon. The Union was dissolved. When the news reached Watertown, everyone was concerned. The war was all anyone could talk about. Anti-slavery sermons were preached at all the churches and war meetings were held throughout the city. Shortly after war was declared, recruiting offices were set up in Watertown and eager young men began to volunteer to fight for their country.

WATERTOWN RIFLE COMPANY AT MESS. This c. 1861 photograph shows one of the Civil War units from Watertown partaking of a meal while encamped at Fond du Lac, Wisconsin. (Watertown Historical Society collection.)

ROSTER FOR COMPANY E, 20TH WISCONSIN VOLUNTEER REGIMENT. This unit from Watertown was made up almost exclusively of German residents. (Watertown Historical Society collection.)

In April 1861, a company of militia from Minnesota marched through Watertown en route for the conflict. Their presence led to a strong patriotic fervor in the city and a public meeting was held soon after to raise funds to provide for the families of those who enlisted in the army. The patriotic zeal ran high in young and old alike. In one instance of rampant patriotism, a son of Mayor William M. Dennis scared the wits out of his family by climbing to the very top of the family home and nailing the stars and stripes to the gable end of the house.

The first of four military companies, the Watertown Rifles, was organized in Watertown in April 1861. Their headquarters were in the Chappell Block on West Main Street. Volunteers wore red, white, and blue rosettes, which were presented to them by the ladies of Watertown. On May 12, the men were issued their first uniforms and allotted to the Third Regiment as Company A.

Their headquarters were then transferred to the Mud Tavern on West Main Street, about a mile west of the heart of town. This former Sommergarten was then renamed Camp Bertram after Henry Bertram who managed the complex and also served in the company. A private in this company wrote the editor of the *Watertown Democrat* enthusiastically about life in the camp: "Our location . . . is on beautiful grounds . . . we could not be more pleasantly situated and we have all the comforts of our . . . homes." This same writer went on to describe the daily regimen of camp life and the officers:

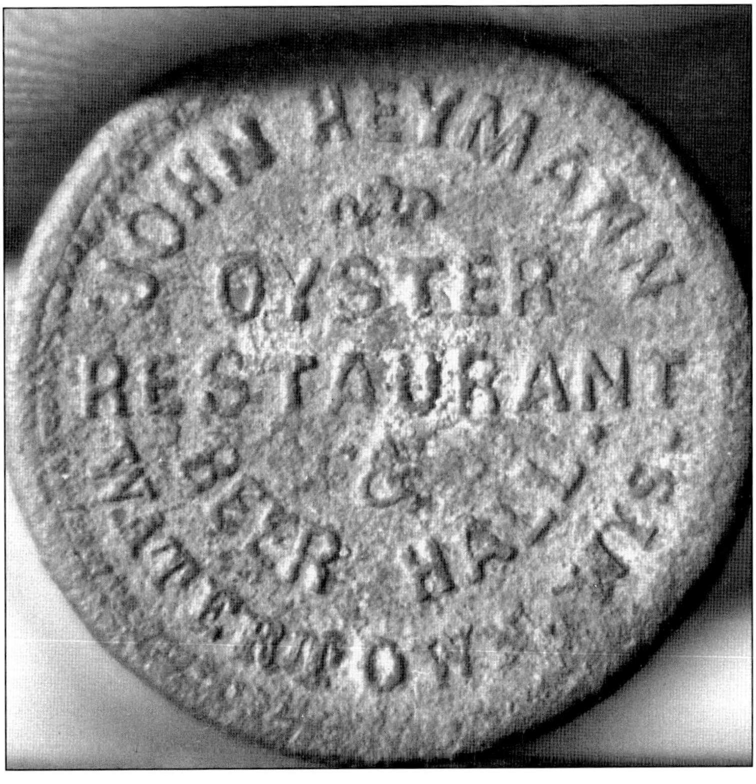

HARD-TIMES TOKEN. In 1863 the United States suffered from a money shortage and most businesses, including those in Watertown, issued their own currency. This token was found on a Civil War battlefield and is now in the Watertown Historical Society's collection.

> Our daily camp duties are . . . Reveille at 5:00 AM; Breakfast at 7:00 . . . 8:30 "Guard Mounting" . . . at 9:00 "drill call" . . . 12:00 dinner . . . 2:00 drill till 4:00 . . . Retreat is beat at 6:00, supper and amusements till 9:00; 15 minutes after everyone is *supposed* to be in bed and lights extinguished.

In June, the company received orders to report to their regiment at Fond du Lac and there be sworn in. Just before they left, the Reverend Charles Boynton of the Congregational Church preached a farewell sermon of encouragement to the troop, and they were off. It was then that stern reality hit the young volunteers. Two months of camp life, the realities of war, and the prospects of leaving wives and sweethearts tested the mettle of the men and a rash of desertions took place. Some simply refused to be sworn in and returned home. Others ran off. One man, with a bounty of $30 on his head, was caught near his father's home in Johnson Creek and taken back to Fond du Lac in chains, but such cases were the exception rather than the norm.

THE HABHEGGER SOMMERGARTEN. This was the site of the "battle of Habhegger's bridge," which took place in Watertown in 1863. (Watertown Historical Society collection.)

GRAND ARMY OF THE REPUBLIC REUNION, C. 1893. This photograph was taken during a reunion of Watertown veterans of the Civil War. (Watertown Historical Society collection.)

Back home, patriotism and profiteering began working hand in hand. In May 1861, the employees of the Milwaukee and Western Railroad raised a flagstaff 100 feet near their machine shop and hung a banner from it measuring 30 feet by 18 feet. A committee of ladies hoisted it aloft and sang the "Star-Spangled Banner" to deafening cheers.

Also in May, the firm of Fischer and Rohr, a tailoring establishment, were awarded a government contract to furnish uniforms for the Watertown Rifle Company. In June, Henry Bertram and J.H. Meyer were each awarded contracts to provide shoes for the soldiers. Andrew Peterson at this time used the war as a basis for an advertisement of his store in the *Watertown Democrat*, which read as follows: "Secession! Secession! War Expected! Fort Sumter Surrendered And A. Peterson Has Fortified Himself With A Large Stock Bought For Cash At Panic Prices!"

In June, Governor Alexander W. Randall requested that the ladies of Watertown make 500 flannel shirts for soldiers, which they delivered in a record five days. Bibles were also purchased by the citizens of Watertown and presented to the departing troops.

Company A of the Third Wisconsin Regiment, which included the Watertown Rifles, passed through the city in July on their way to Elmira, New York, where they would get their arms and equipment. At that time, the regiment numbered 1,011 officers and men. The regiment was assigned to look after the Maryland legislature and they also took a prominent part in the battle of Bolivar Heights in October. Captain Henry Bertram headed this regiment and soon after the Bolivar Heights battle, he was promoted to the rank of lieutenant colonel of the 20th Wisconsin Regiment.

Meanwhile, things were far from quiet at home in Watertown. In the summer of 1861, there was a rumor of a Native American uprising. Word spread that a group of Native Americans had killed several citizens in the town of Kekoskee and they were supposedly headed towards Watertown. A group of townspeople gathered along the North Fourth Street bridge to await the deadly foe, but this proved to be a false alarm. The only fatality of this supposed massacre was that of a pig.

In the fall of 1861, the second volunteer company to be raised in Watertown was formed. This company, which would later become Company D of the 16th Wisconsin, was called the Union Guards and Captain Oliver D. Pease formed it. After remaining in camp at Madison for several weeks, this company received its order to move down the Mississippi and, on April 1, 1862, it was encamped at Savannah, Tennessee. Pease was killed in 1862 at the battle of Pittsburgh Landing near Shiloh. Besides Pease, the company lost six others. Captain Pease's body

CONRAD DIPPLE. Known as "One-Armed" Dipple after losing his arm in the Civil War, he later served as a school teacher in Watertown. (Watertown Historical Society collection.)

HENRY BASSINGER. This celebrated character lived to be 101 years old despite never drinking a glass of pure water after seeing bloated horses in a stream during the Civil War.

was sent home and he was buried with full honors. The local Grand Army of the Republic (GAR) Post 94 was named in his honor. The Union Guards would continue to take part in many of the hard-fought battles, including the battle of Corinth. In the words of one historian, it "aided materially in putting down the rebellion."

By December of 1861, the *Watertown Democrat* was able to write, "There is a large sprinkling of military uniforms in our streets just now. Nearly every other man one meets is a soldier." Thus, the first year of the conflict drew to a close. Patriotism was still high in Watertown, but as the war wore on, ideals and outlooks would change.

The year 1862 began on a sour note. A disastrous fire swept through downtown Watertown, very nearly destroying a good section of Main Street between Second and Third Streets. Were it not for a shopkeeper storing dynamite in the upper story of his building, the whole street may have gone up. As it was, the fire struck this building, ignited the dynamite, and the building exploded, creating a firebreak. Thus, the street was saved.

THE LEWIS CIVIL WAR MONUMENT. Dedicated in 1899, this monument was a gift to the city of Watertown by Mr. and Mrs. George B. Lewis. (Watertown Historical Society collection.)

More men were needed and another company was organized, this one being the Watertown German Volunteers. The company was organized on August 11, 1862 and on August 15, it became Company E of the 20th Wisconsin. This company numbered 106 volunteers and was comprised mostly of young men residing in Watertown. At noon on August 16, a large body of citizens escorted the troops to the depot where they took the train to Madison. Newly appointed Lieutenant Colonel Henry Bertram and Captain John Weber led the men, most whom were members of the local Turnerverein, a gymnastic group that was founded in Watertown in 1860.

Not to be out-done by the Germans, an Irish Company was founded in August as well and was but partially filled by citizens of Watertown, owing to a large number of Irish having previously enlisted in other companies. Valentine Sweeney and Dr. Edward Johnson recruited this troop. The Watertown Irish Company, or the Irish Brigade as it came to be known, became Company D of the 17th Wisconsin Volunteers and it rendered invaluable service in many of the greatest battles of the rebellion.

Dr. Johnson has the distinction of being the first druggist in Watertown, coming to the city in 1844. He also created the very first soda fountain in the state. He was a fierce supporter of the Union and, as proof of this, one has only to look at what happened when someone, as a joke, hung the Confederate flag over his store. Johnson took one look at it, ran inside, fetched his ax, cut it down, and threatened to do the same to anyone who dared to pull such a stunt again!

On September 2, 1862, the Watertown American Volunteer Company was organized. This company was, according to one history, "comprised of some of the best citizens of Watertown" and it later became Company B, 29th Wisconsin Regiment. The company received its marching orders and left Camp Randall in Madison on November 2 and headed south. The troop arrived in Helena, Arkansas on November 6 and remained there until April 1863.

In December 1862, the German company took a distinguished part in the desperate battle of Prairie Grove, Arkansas. Six men were killed in this battle and Lieutenant Colonel Bertram had a horse shot out from beneath him. Captain John Weber was wounded in this battle and later died of his injuries. The company pursued the rebels to Van Buren, Arkansas, where 800 prisoners, 2 steamers, and a ferryboat loaded with provisions were captured.

Also in December, the citizens of Watertown received an unusual Christmas present in the form of a 70-pound bell from the Watertown boys fighting in Mississippi. The bell, which was sent to Bernard O'Byrne, was accompanied with the following note:

> This bell was achieved by the 29th Wis. Regt. on a deserted plantation in the state of Mississippi. Its former owner is in rebellion against his government—founded on the virtue and intelligence of the people. It was wont to arouse slaves to unrequited toil; let it now call freemen to duty.

And so ended 1862.

The year 1863 was a year of insurrection as far as the home front was concerned. Spirits began to flag and a sudden rash of anti-war and anti-Lincoln feelings began to manifest themselves in the heart of many of the citizens of Watertown. These dissenters were called "copperheads" and they took to wearing badges that denoted their feelings.

The unrest first began to show itself in March when word began to spread throughout the city that Mayor William Dennis had used his influence to procure arms from the state for use by a military company to be commanded by Captain Leonard Jaehrling. The editor of the *Watertown Republican* insisted that this troop's real purpose was to resist the coming military draft and to kill off "damned black Republicans." The mayor, of course, refuted this charge.

In the summer of 1863, a courier came to Watertown with the news that an enrolling officer was headed to the city to take down the names of those who were eligible for the draft. This so outraged the copperheads in the city that they quickly assembled and, with their muskets on their shoulders, started for the scene. These volunteers wore no uniforms and did not show any soldierly discipline or bearing as they marched through Main Street and turned north to the scene of the outrage that they were so eager to suppress. After they marched for about a mile, they came upon the North Fourth Street bridge, but more importantly they came upon John Habhegger's saloon located near it. There they stopped to assuage their thirst with a glass or two of beer. While they were tossing a few back, they were met by another courier with the news that seven soldiers armed with rifles were escorting the enrollment officer. This was cold news. What could they do? The mob compromised over a few more glasses of beer and marched back into the city. Nothing more was said of the matter.

A draft drawing was held on November 12, 1863 in Janesville and a large number of Jefferson County citizens were present. There were 278 names from Watertown in the wheel and 40 names were drawn. This draft was met with a certain amount of resistance. The draft came again and, on September 22, 1864, the Third and Seventh Wards of Watertown fell under the draft at this time, the other wards of the city having filled their quotas by enlistment. A supplemental draft was held on October 15, 1864 in the Seventh Ward. It was announced at that time that supplemental drafts would be held in every sub-district until the full quota of each was full. "If those first drawn run away or are rejected," a newspaper reported, "this process will go on indefinitely."

In May 1863, news came through that General Ulysses S. Grant had fought five successive battles and gained as many decisive victories over the rebels in Vicksburg and there was great rejoicing in Watertown. The brass band came out and paraded the streets, salutes were fired, and a general feeling of delight could be read in almost every face.

But there was still a war on and battles to be fought and won. In January 1864, the Watertown American Company were engaged in many important battles, including the storming of Spanish Fort near Mobile, Alabama where two men of

RACING TO THE FIRE. This image shows the fire engine from the Phoenix Fire Co. on North Water Street responding to a call, c. 1895. During the Civil War there were two disastrous fires that nearly wiped out Main Street.

the company were captured. Those captured were Private Porter Gibbs, brother of Captain Darius Gibbs, and musician Allen J. Rutherford, who had the distinction of being one of the youngest volunteer soldiers from Wisconsin. He was only 13 years old at the time he enlisted.

Because of the length of the war, many men were ending their hitches in the service and it once again became necessary to open recruiting offices in Watertown. One opened in December 1863, another in January 1864, and a third one opened in February 1864. The new incentives to joining the army were the bounty payments being paid to soldiers who enlisted. By July 1864, Watertown had filled her quota under the call for 500,000 volunteers.

Weary of the war, the calendar turned to 1865 and with it came the joyous news of the fall of Richmond on April 10 and General Robert E. Lee's surrender shortly thereafter. The reaction in Watertown was quiet at first. A crowd gathered around the Bank of Watertown at First and Main Streets and they listened to A.L. Pritchard read the news. When he finished, he called for three cheers for the war heroes and the crowd reacted with a mighty roar. Then, he asked for three cheers for the President, but the crowd barely reacted. Lincoln was still viewed by many of the copperheads in Watertown as a villain and they had gone so far as to hire thugs to try and prevent people from voting for his re-election in the previous year.

After this, the celebration began in earnest. Bonfires were set up in the streets and all residences were lit up. Main Street was filled with people and a grand procession paraded from one end of the street to the other and back again, with banners flying, music playing, and the multitude shouting themselves hoarse.

Liquor flowed like water throughout the day and as night descended, people became less choosy about what they drank. All of this excess brought out the worst in the celebrants and many fights broke out. One notable conflict took place between John Manning and a German tailor. Manning insulted the tailor by calling him a "damned dutchman" and the tailor retaliated by grabbing Manning's coattails and ripping his coat up the back. Manning had to high tail it out of there on horseback in order to escape the outraged tailor.

The celebration ended on a sour note when Colonel Charles Gill got up on the balcony of Cole's Hall on Main Street and addressed the crowd. Gill had few friends in Watertown since he served as school superintendent in the 1850s and proved to be very strict with the teachers and students under his command. He exuberantly alluded to the fact that a troop of African Americans commanded by General Weitzel had been the first to enter Richmond. Gill yelled to the crowd that the south deserved the humiliation and he ended his tirade by shouting that "a brigade of n——rs commanded by a Dutchman" had been the first Union troops the rebels saw in that city. This remark cast a coolness over the proceedings and after a few feeble attempts to sing the national anthem, the crowd disbursed.

Sadly, the joy felt over the end of the war was quickly overshadowed by the news of Lincoln's assassination a few days later. When the word reached Watertown, it was said that strong men stopped what they were doing and wept openly. Stores closed and from every pulpit in the city, sermons of praise to the soul of Abraham Lincoln were heard. One of the largest of the many observances was held at the Congregational church, where the church bell tolled for the martyred president.

On July 5, the 29th Wisconsin Regiment returned home and were given a royal fete. A reception was held July 13 to honor the returning war heroes. When all was said and done, it was estimated that Watertown sent about 700 men to war. Of these, 150 were sent home on disability, 200 were discharged at the end of the war, and the balance died in combat or from other causes.

No one ever forgot the war or their service. Many men were referred to by their military rank forever afterwards, such as General Henry Bertram or Captain Fred Kusel. Others were reminded of the war by their lost limbs, such as Conrad Dipple, known as "One Armed Dipple." He lost his arm near Pittsburgh, Pennsylvania. He came back to Watertown and worked as a schoolteacher. Another man, known as "Peg Leg Griep," lost his leg at Gettysburg. He was wont to tell the harrowing tale of his battlefield amputation by saying that the surgeon sawed his leg off with no anesthetic except "a lot of good strong moonshine whiskey."

Still others were changed mentally by the war, such as Henry Bassinger who never drank a drop of pure water after seeing dead horses lying in a stream when he was fetching water for his camp. The sight so sickened him that he swore off water for good and lived to the astonishing age of 101!

Then there is the case of Major Charles Gardner. He was born in St. Petersburg, Russia and came to Watertown in 1846. When war broke out, he left town and headed for Missouri where he enlisted in the Confederate army. He rose to the rank of cavalry major and fought till the end of the war. When he returned to Watertown, he was not very popular. A group of boys dragged him down to the river and beat him up for his unreconstructed Southern views. Despite this, he went to work and earned enough money as an agent for a reaper company to study law at Madison. After graduating, he returned to Watertown and was elected the city attorney. He was regarded as an able lawyer and would have gone further had he not drowned while fishing on Lac LaBelle in 1904.

The war was never forgotten in Watertown and as a testimonial to the brave men who fought and died for the United States, a monument was erected in the Veteran's Park in 1899; it was given to the city by Mr. and Mrs. George B. Lewis. Across the street from this monument today is the home of the nationally known First Brigade Band, an authentic recreation of a Civil War brass band. Somehow that seems fitting.

WATERTOWN BRASS BAND. This c. 1863 image shows one of the brass bands that was made up of Watertown men during the Civil War.

6. From Darkness into the Light: 1865–1890

Watertown, with her large German population, is more like a sister city to Milwaukee than any other in the Badger State. Milwaukeeans visit Watertown and feel as much at home with the good-hearted, hospitable and entertaining Watertownians as they would in partaking of the good cheer "zwei lager und blenty bologna" which abounds here.

Watertown Democrat, June 17, 1875

After the end of the Civil War, Watertown entered into a period of quiet desperation. The reason? The horrible realization of the consequences of the railroad bond fiasco. Since the beginnings of the 1860s, the bonds were part and parcel of each election. Every candidate pledged to remove the city from the mess it was in, but no one ever seemed entirely capable of actually doing anything.

The bond case is difficult to relate, since it is so very complicated. Simply put, during the time just after the depression of 1857 and for many years afterwards, people, fearing that their investments would be wiped out, began to sell their bonds for a fraction of their value to a handful of out-of-town speculators who proceeded to hold the city for ransom for the next 30 years. One of these speculators was from Milwaukee and he made a business of buying up bonds when they were listed as low as 8¢ or 10¢ on the dollar. As a result of this, potential businesses that might have otherwise considered Watertown a prime location tended to shy away from the city out of uncertainty over the bond situation. Watertown may have been the second largest city in Wisconsin before 1857 but by the 1870s, its growth and potential had been stunted. This situation would plague the city for many years to come.

The city tried to reason with the railroads and the Chicago & Northwestern Line agreed to redeem its bonds by offering an equivalent amount of stock. But the Milwaukee & Madison line refused to negotiate. This firm had been sold to new owners and they had no intention of honoring bonds issued by former owners. To make matters worse, speculators began to demand payments in full from the city on the bonds that they held. One speculator boasted that he added 10 percent interest every year to the total amount of the bonds that he owned.

A group of citizens formed a Debt Association in 1867 to come to some sort of an agreement with the bondholders. One of the members of this committee was Daniel Hall, a prominent Watertown lawyer. He was elected to the state legislature in 1870 and secured the passage of a bill authorizing a commission to negotiate with the bondholders. The bonded debt of the city at this time, principal and interest, amounted to $750,000. The assessed value of real estate and personal property in the city was valued at $1.5 million.

The bondholders were invited to a meeting and Hall offered to pay 50 percent of the principal in 15 annual installments at 7 percent interest. A small percentage of the debt was extinguished on these terms. However, speculators who had bought their bonds for a song and held large numbers of them would not agree to this compromise; thus, the bond scandal began to escalate.

RAILROAD BOND COFFIN. *This photograph shows one of the little coffins that were placed on the doorsteps of prominent Watertown citizens on June 19, 1872. Each coffin bore a message warning the recipients to bury their bonds in the coffins. (Watertown Historical Society collection.)*

THE GREAT SNOWSTORM OF 1881. This image was captured on March 8, 1881 and shows a mountain of snow along Main Street between Fourth and Fifth Streets.

Daniel Hall immediately persuaded the state legislators to pass a unique law that held federal marshals at bay. The scheme worked like this: a mayor and seven aldermen, elected in the usual way, would meet secretly, qualify for office, determine the tax levy for the following year, and then resign. Seven elected senior aldermen, really street commissioners who could not tax or represent the city legally, would then take over the management of city affairs. Thus, the city ran without a proper form of city government for the next 20 years. Watertown would not revert to normal governing until 1894.

Meanwhile, on a local level, violent opposition had been growing among the residents of Watertown over the Debt Association and its plan for compromising the debt. A radical group known as the Union League was founded in 1872 and was lead by "half a dozen rabble-rousers." This group would stymie all efforts of the city to try to resolve the indebtedness and control politics in Watertown for years. The league refused to consider anything but outright repudiation. They accused the Debt Association leaders of buying up bonds to enrich themselves.

On the night of June 19, 1872, five little black coffins were placed on the doorsteps of five Watertown residences. In each was a slip of paper upon which was written, "In this bury all your railway bonds and your villainy with it. Beware." The only problem was, none of the persons to whom the coffins were addressed was a holder of any bonds!

The Union League obstructed the city's prosperity and growth during the 15 years it was in existence and made Watertown's name a joke in the state. They held protest meetings in which speakers threatened the destruction of all railway property in the city. Patrick Devy, the hot-headed leader of the league, stated on one occasion that he was in favor of making "a pile of ashes of the city" to see what the "cruel bondholders" would then do to collect their money.

In 1874, the league got control of the city council and elected Hezikiah Flinn as mayor. Flinn appeared on the platform with a huge stick and announced, "I don't know enough about the fine arts of office . . . but there is one thing I do know, and that is that I don't care a damn for all the railroads and all the bondholders in the country!"

THE ICE VELOCIPEDE. Invented in 1888 by Watertown inventor Julius Schemmel, this machine was the forerunner to the modern snowmobile.

THEODORE BERNHARD. This pioneer educator established the first free textbooks in Wisconsin in 1877, as well as the first high school in Watertown. (Watertown Historical Society collection.)

The stalemate in the city continued. As late as 1884, four marshals were in Watertown after an election, but the mood of the populace was such that none of them could have successfully served a warrant. Then, in 1889, the Supreme Court handed down a decision on the case that outlawed every bond that had not been reduced to a judgment, and most of the bondholders gave up. Ephraim Mariner, a Milwaukee lawyer and bond speculator, accepted $15,000 in exchange for bonds and judgments totalling $600,000. On the day the news of the decision arrived, the city broke out into a spontaneous celebration.

But it was premature, as one persistent bondholder, E.W. Metcalf, appealed his case once more and the Supreme Court allowed his claim on a technicality. Watertown was directed to pay him $35,000 in 20 annual installments. When the final payment was made in 1905, the city once again celebrated with a great parade, led by Mayor Herman Wertheimer, who carried a broom as a symbol that the city had at last swept away its debt.

Thus ended the blackest period in Watertown's history.

As if all of this wasn't bad enough, in March 1881, the city experienced one of the harshest snowstorms ever seen. Over 6 feet of snow was dumped on the city, cutting it off from the outside world for several days. Tunnels were dug in order to get across Main Street and trains were stalled on the tracks. The snow in some places measured 22 feet deep. Life was difficult during the snowstorm and many people recalled that food and fuel were scarce. Temperatures began to rise not long after the storm struck and, by the end of the month, things had improved. But the melting snow caused flooding and when the ice floes from the northern part of the city began to break up, they tore out the Main Street bridge. The terrible winters in the 1880s spawned local inventor Julius Schemmel to invent a precursor to the snowmobile which he named the "Ice Velocipede" in 1888. This contraption resembled a high-wheeled bike on skis.

Despite the crippling effects of the bond scandal on the city, life in Watertown still went on. Actually, in examining the records, one is amazed at how much the city managed to achieve during this bleak time. What happened in Watertown is an illustration of the old adage that says what you cannot do for yourself, you manage to find a way to do for your children. For example, in 1877, the first free textbooks in the state were issued in Watertown. This was a scheme of Theodore Bernhard, the leading educator in the city. Prior to this, textbooks had to be purchased by the parents of students for use in the schools. By issuing free textbooks, education was made available to rich and poor alike. In 1883, the first high school was built in Watertown and this building joined the other Union

NORTHWESTERN UNIVERSITY (LATER COLLEGE), C. 1880. This Lutheran institution of higher learning was established in Watertown in 1863.

Schools in the city. The other schools in Watertown at this time were Union School #1, built in 1863 and located on East Main Street, Union School #2, built in 1867 and located on North Montgomery Street, and Union School #3, built in 1871 and located on Lincoln Street.

Two colleges also opened during this period, Northwestern University (later renamed Northwestern College) and Our Lady of the Sacred Heart College. Both of these schools were religion oriented, Northwestern being affiliated with the Lutheran church and Sacred Heart being Catholic.

Northwestern College opened in a small building located on North Fourth Street in 1863 and it was originally known as Wisconsin University. The main focus of the college was the training of young men for the ministry. By the end of the 1860s, the college had moved its campus to Western Avenue and began to greatly expand. In later years, the seminary program was dropped and the school became a private liberal arts college. In 1994, Northwestern College transferred its college classes to New Ulm, Minnesota and the Watertown campus became a Lutheran high school, today known as Martin Luther Preparatory School, or Luther Prep as Watertown people call it.

The Brothers of the Holy Cross founded Sacred Heart in 1872. The school was located on West Main Street, on the former farmstead owned by Patrick Rogan. It opened as a private Catholic college with a regular college course curriculum and it was chartered in 1874. Sacred Heart was in operation until 1886 when the brothers converted it to a normal school for their members. In 1889, it again

SACRED HEART COLLEGE. *Established in 1872, this was a Catholic college run by the Brothers of the Holy Cross. Today it is the site of Maranatha Baptist Bible College.*

WISCONSIN DAIRYMEN'S ASSOCIATION MARKER. In 1872, in the Lindon House hotel in Watertown, a group of dairymen founded this association, the first of its kind in the state. This marker on the Watertown Public Library, where the Lindon House once stood, commemorates this important event. (Watertown Historical Society collection.)

became a regular Catholic college. In 1912, the college was converted to a high school–age seminary for young men who were interested in joining the Holy Cross Fathers. The seminary operated until 1955 when the Holy Cross Fathers converted the facility into a military academy. In 1968, the campus was sold to officials of the Baptist church and since that time, it has been the site of Maranatha Baptist Bible College.

On February 15, 1872, a group of Wisconsin dairy farmers met in the Lindon House hotel in Watertown to form the Wisconsin Dairymen's Association, headed by W.D. Hoard of Fort Atkinson, owner and editor of the *Jefferson County Union* and later *Hoard's Dairyman* magazine. This association helped to attract attention to the heretofore little thought-of dairy industry and it helped establish Wisconsin as the leading dairy producing state in the United States. Several cheese factories and dairy plants began to open in the Watertown area during the last half of the nineteenth century. Notable amongst the early dairy pioneers were the Habhegger and Jossi families, immigrants from Switzerland, who were reportedly the first to manufacture Swiss cheese in Wisconsin. The Habheggers and Jossis later went on to operate cold storage plants, which lasted well into the twentieth century. Other dairies included the Jahnke Creamery on Western Avenue, the Brinkman Dairy, McFarland Dairy, Indra Dairy, Kasten Dairy, Kraemer's, and Mullen's. The latter two firms are still in existence, though they are primarily retail outlets today.

Agriculture increased during this time and the J.B. Bennett Company in Watertown began to manufacture a reaper that would greatly ease the workload on the farmer. The Bennett Company went out of existence in 1890 and its factory was taken over by the Ernst Kunert (later Dornfeldt-Kunert) Company. The Kunert Company specialized in the manufacture of bridges, brewer's equipment, boilers, and engines. This firm lasted through the early days of the twentieth century.

On a governmental level, despite the lack of proper leadership, the city managed to build an impressive and imposing city hall building in 1885. Prior to this, city offices were located on the southeastern corner of Main and First Streets. This building also housed the city post office as well.

In addition, a new fire department was organized in the city in 1876. This came about as a result of the city being faced with the decision of having to choose between two fire engines. The city needed a new machine for its Pioneer Engine Company and two separate engines were sent to the city for its approval. Each was run through a battery of tests and each proved to be, more or less, up to the challenges that were thrown at it.

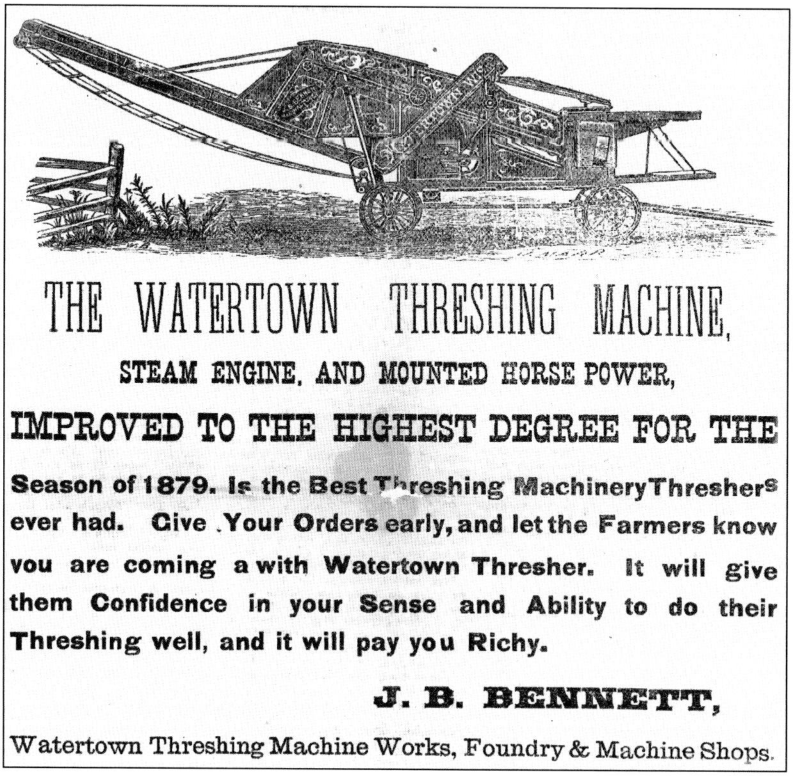

AD FOR WATERTOWN THRESHING MACHINE. *This ad, which appeared in the* Watertown Republican *on July 30, 1879, touted the advantages of this thresher, made by the J.B. Bennett Co. of Watertown.*

THE ERNST KUNERT COMPANY. This c. 1890 image shows the E. Kunert Co., a manufacturer of bridges and metal products.

The city officials, faced with a tough decision, created a committee to look into the matter. This committee, in turn, created a sub-committee. After reviewing the machines and running them through yet another battery of tests, the sub-committee deferred to the main committee, who, in turn, passed the buck to the city council. It was decision time and the city council decided that since each had their strengths, that they would purchase both so that there could be a firefighting force on the west side of the river as well as the east side. Thus, in 1876, the Phoenix Fire Company was founded. These two companies would serve the city until 1912 when the two companies were merged into one entity.

Other city improvements included the introduction of telephone service in 1877 and the arrival of electricity in 1889. The first telephone was installed in 1877 by John B. May, a local photographer, who ran a line from his office on Main Street to Turner Hall. By 1881, May began the telephone exchange in Watertown and a 30-member switchboard was installed in his office. Telephone number one was installed in the Globe Milling office, a fact of which the company was very proud. May later sold his telephone service to the newly formed Watertown Telephone Company. This concern had offices for a time at 101 East Main Street on the upper floor and, in 1927, the telephone company moved to a new building on South Fourth Street where it remains today.

The electric company in Watertown began as the Watertown Electric Light Company. At first, the company operated a small steam generating plant for electricity. The city was lighted by electricity for the first time on

December 2, 1889, prompting the *Watertown Gazette* to write the following on December 6, 1889:

> The city was lighted for the first time last Monday night with electric light. At first a little difficulty was had in getting the light to work properly, but on Tuesday and Wednesday nights the light worked to perfection, which speaks well for the Thomson-Housten system and the Watertown Electric Light Co. in getting it so promptly in shape on the night advertised. It is as good a light as any we have seen in any city, and better than some. We feel justified in claiming this, as we have probably seen as many cities lighted by electric light as any person in the city. It is equal to the light of Eau Claire, Steven's Point, Madison, Oshkosh and LaCrosse in this state, and to that of the cities of Peoria, Bloomington, Pekin, Joliet, and other cities we have visited in Illinois. The only fault we find is with the Board of Street Commissioners in not ordering more placed in sections of the city not now lighted by either gas or electric light.

WATERTOWN CITY HALL. This was the site of the seat of city government in Watertown from 1871 to 1885. It also housed the post office. (Gerald Kreitzman collection.)

In 1902, the company was purchased by the Watertown Electric Company. They acquired the former Rough & Ready dam site located along South Concord Avenue in the eastern part of the city and, in 1903, the dam was rebuilt. In 1909, the dam site was again improved and a large generating plant was erected. The interurban trolley line that ran through the city later acquired this generating plant and, by the 1940s, this building was abandoned. As of this writing, the building still stands empty.

In 1905, the gas and electric company merged to form the Watertown Gas and Electric Company and afterwards this firm was acquired by the Wisconsin Gas and Electric Company, who established offices on the corner of Main and Third Streets in a former saloon. The Wisconsin Electric Company, the present firm, provides electrical service to the city. The office on Main Street in Watertown was closed in the early 1990s and all business is currently conducted out of Milwaukee.

Industry continued to evolve and change through this period. The pioneer industries, such as flour milling and sawmilling, the iron foundry founded in the 1850s, and the woolen mill begun in the 1840s continued to decline through the end of the 1800s and, by 1900, most were gone. For example, at the beginning of the 1870s, there were five flour mills in operation with an aggregate of 22 run of stones and a grinding capacity of about 300 barrels of flour daily. By the turn of the century, however, there were only two mills still in operation, the Globe Mill on the west side of the Rock River and the Koenig Mill on South First Street. By the end of the 1950s, only the Globe Mill was still in operation. In May 2001, this mill, which had stood empty since the end of the 1980s, burned to the ground, effectively removing all traces of the once dominant milling business from the city landscape.

The cigar business was on the upswing. By the 1870s, there were five cigar factories in the city, the largest being the Wiggenhorn Brothers, which proved to be a training ground for most of the other cigar makers in Watertown. The industry had been founded by a pair of "Latin Farmers," Emil Rothe (a firebrand lawyer) and Theodore Bernhard (a prominent educator) in the 1850s. Their small concern, however, was not a success and soon closed. In 1858, Eugene Wiggenhorn opened a small factory, which grew to become the second largest enterprise in Wisconsin. In 1880 alone, the combined products of Watertown's cigar makers were 2 million cigars. Other firms in the city included the Wilkowski Brothers, Schleuter Brothers, A.F. Miller and Company, and William Schimmel. By the 1940s, cigar making had all but ceased and by the 1960s, the processing of tobacco, an outgrowth of the cigar industry, had faded from Watertown's industrial scene as well.

The G.B. Lewis Company was in full swing at this time. They owned a large sash and blind factory located along South Water Street along the riverfront. The factory would increase in size and in the early 1900s, after a disastrous fire, it switched its manufacturing output from wooden boxes and other products to the manufacture of beekeeping supplies. In the 1930s, the company created the

"Arki-toy," which was a sort of cross between an Erector Set and Lincoln Logs, and during the 1940s, it manufactured airplane propellers. After World War II, it became a pioneer in the manufacturing of fiberglass products. The firm passed through several different hands before going out of business in 2001.

Other industries begun in the latter half of the nineteenth century that would continue and expand in the twentieth and twenty-first centuries included the Watertown Table Slide Company and the Brandt Automatic Cashier Company. The Blaesius Brothers founded the Table Slide Company in 1889. This firm created the metal housings that allowed for tables to be pulled apart and extra leaves inserted. Former employees of the Watertown Table Slide Company formed a rival firm, the Perfection Table Slide Company, in Watertown in 1924. This firm passed out of existence in 1953. By 1954, the Watertown Table Slide Company was one of only five companies in the United States to manufacture both standard and specially sized table slides at their factory.

Local bank teller and inventor Edward J. Brandt founded the Brandt Automatic Cashier Company in 1894. This firm made coin counting machines, which eased the lives of bank tellers and other individuals who had to count large numbers of coins. De La Rue Industries absorbed the Brandt Company in the 1990s. Though no longer locally owned, it is one of the few industries that has remained relatively unchanged up to the present time.

It is to Watertown's credit that as each industry declines and disappears from the landscape, others have taken their place. The city is not dependent on any one major industry for its economic well being. Thus, Watertown has the ability and advantage of being able to constantly reinvent itself.

Watertown's commercial district underwent changes at this time as well. Most frame buildings were being replaced by imposing brick structures throughout the period. There was still an eclectic mix of small stores along Main Street, but some, such as the Schempf Brothers store, were becoming larger, with a bigger and better selection of goods. They were becoming department stores. By 1903, the Schempf Brothers' "Big Cash" Store would become the largest and most patronized department store in the city.

In order to compete with firms like Schempf's, other stores began to specialize in certain lines of goods. Millinery shops, shoe stores, stationery stores, drug stores, candy stores, bakeries, all a part of the make-up of Main Street, now began to flourish. With specialty shops and department stores on the rise, the general stores began to decline and all but disappeared after the turn of the century. By the end of the 1890s, Watertown's Main Street was a large and thriving commercial district that not only drew trade from the city, but also attracted customers from rural areas.

Finally, the second half of the nineteenth century was an era where social and recreational activities became more accepted. New technology allowed people the luxury of more free time to enjoy pursuits other than work. Many churches in the city sponsored groups and clubs that provided an outlet for group activities, and there were several fraternal organizations in the city as well, such as the Masons

WATERTOWN'S "NEW" CITY HALL. Erected in 1885, this was the seat of Watertown city government until 1965 when a new municipal building was erected. On this site today is a very picturesque parking lot. (Watertown Historical Society collection.)

and Odd Fellows Lodges. In 1860, the German residents of the city organized a gymnastic or Turner association, which is still active. Not only did the local Turnerverein stress physical development, it also offered a performance space and fostered political debates.

With the construction of the Turner Opera House in 1868, Watertown had its first permanent theater and the residents of the city were treated to traveling theatrical troupes, lectures, singers, and other celebrities of the day. Prior to the erection of Turner Hall, plays or lectures were presented at public halls, churches, or large rooms in the city's many hotels.

In 1888, the second permanent theater was constructed in Watertown when the Concordia Musical Society built their grand opera house on North First Street across from the city hall. The Concordia Opera House was a sumptuous structure that reportedly held 600 seats. In addition, the Concordia Society also purchased a small island on the east side of the city at this time and fixed it up, adding a large fountain, graveled paths and a dance pavilion. Concordia Island proved to be a favorite spot for summer picnics and dances and the annual end of school celebrations. The society began a gradual decline through the latter half of the 1890s and, by the early 1900s, it ceased operations. Concordia Island was sold to private individuals who renamed the island Tivoli Island after the hanging gardens of Tivoli. By the 1950s, the buildings were destroyed. The island today is a nature preserve. As for the opera house, after serving as a vaudeville theater and movie house, it was sold in 1916 to the local Elks Club who use it today as their meeting place.

THE PHOENIX FIRE COMPANY. Built in 1876 on North Water Street, this was the second fire company formed in Watertown. It merged with the Pioneer Engine Company in 1912. (Watertown Historical Society collection.)

7. Into the New Century: 1890–1900

The city . . . has added to her improvements. Sewers have been laid, waterworks built, and the dark cloud which hung over the city from 1853 to 1894, namely, the railroad bonds, has been settled so that Watertown can now come forth in an independent manhood to invite capital and labor and go on in the march of progress in a manner which nature meant she should. The city is a small empire within itself, and her attainments show wonderful vitality when one considers her handicapped conditions for many years past.

A.I. Lord, *The Industrial Review of Watertown*, Wisconsin, 1897

With the long nightmare of the bond scandal behind it, the city of Watertown entered the 1890s determined to make up for lost time. To that end, city services began to be created during this time. The most important of these services was the establishment of proper sewer and water systems.

In 1894, the city began construction of a sewerage system. As stated earlier, the city had a rudimentary sewer system in place as early as 1855, but a more complex system was laid out in the 1890s. In 1895, the city contracted with a private company to build a waterworks plant and pipeline system, which was then sold to the city. Prior to this, homes and businesses received their water from artesian wells sunk in various spots in the city and along Main Street. Some of these wells contained water rich in minerals, which was considered very healthful. One, located near the railroad tracks, contained water so rich with minerals that if a piece of metal was lowered into it, the metal would become magnetized. On June 3, 1875, the *Watertown Gazette* reported, "Now that beautiful evenings are upon us, if you happen to see a young man near the Magnetic Well throwing his arms wildly around a fair maid, just let him alone. He knows his business. He's only keeping her from falling into the well."

The main plant of the waterworks was built on the site of the former Globe Mill on the end of South First Street. The mill building had burned to the ground in 1894 and moved its base of operations to the west side of the river. The waterworks complex consisted of a pumping house and a small well house. The first water tower, known as the standpipe, was built in about 1896 along Western

CITY COUNCIL MEETING, C. 1900. Watertown was able to re-establish proper city government in 1894 for the first time since the railroad bond scandal began. (Watertown Historical Society collection.)

Avenue below Northwestern College. This tower was replaced with a modern one in the mid-1960s. Today, the city is serviced by four water towers.

In the latter half of the 1890s, with the implementation of running water in most homes and a proper sewer system, the city decided to do something about the condition of its streets. Main Street was a muddy mess during rainy seasons and filled with ruts. The city fathers decided to have the street paved with brick and, by 1899, Main Street was finished. By 1907, the entire business district had paved streets and, by the 1910s, just about all of Watertown had paved streets. These streets would be paved, repaved, widened, resurfaced, and re-resurfaced throughout the years.

Life became more comfortable and with electricity and running water in homes yet more time was freed up for leisure activities and hobbies. Outdoor activities became popular and bicycling became all the rage. Frank Bishop, son of a local photographer, supposedly introduced the bicycle, or velocipede, to Watertown in 1860. By the 1890s, they were seen with increasing frequency on the city streets. William Thomas, a grandson of John Richards, developed his family's old picnic grounds known as Richards' Woods into a public driving park and bicycle races were held there.

Sports, such as baseball and football, began to take off during this period. Baseball, in particular, fast became the most popular pastime. One of the first baseball teams to be formed in the city was the Live Oaks team in 1868. Various teams were formed throughout the 1870s, 1880s, and 1890s. Each college, Northwestern and Sacred Heart, had their own teams and various spirited contests were held between them and between teams from other cities. Many players on Watertown teams went on to make baseball their careers, the most famous being Adrian "Addie" Joss, who played for the Sacred Heart team, and Fred Merkle. Joss went on to play for Cleveland and was a celebrated pitcher. Merkle, on the other hand, though a fine player, unfortunately made an error in the World Series of 1908. He was playing for the New York Giants and during a tense moment of play, a batter came to the plate and hit the ball. Merkle was on base. Once the ball was hit, it looked as though it was all over and Merkle thought the game was in the bag, so he stepped off the base he was safe upon and left the field, only to have the play intercepted, thus causing the Giants to lose to the Chicago Cubs. He was forever branded with the nickname "Bonehead" as a result.

Football took a little longer to establish itself in Watertown. No college teams played the game until the late 1890s. It was felt that the sport was too rough. The *Watertown Gazette*, on November 20, 1895, ran this article:

BICYCLE RACE IN WATERTOWN, C. 1895. It wasn't just team sports like baseball and football that became popular in the late nineteenth century. This bike race drew a large crowd. (Watertown Historical Society collection.)

> Football has been prohibited as a pastime at the Northwestern University by the faculty, at least, so far as games with outside teams is concerned. The management of the club was in hopes of seeking permission for a Thanksgiving Day game, if nothing more, but even this was refused. The objection of the faculty arises over the roughness which sometimes characterizes the sport and the consequent injuring of the players. The banishment of football from the university field causes considerable disappointment among the student-body, as well as among the devotees of the game in the city.

Basketball, which was played in the city as early as 1902, and other sports would not attract the interest of the Watertown sports-going public until much later, and then mainly as school sporting events. The addition of sports to the public school curriculum happened in the early 1900s. The Watertown public school teams are known as the Goslings. The reason for this quaint appellation comes from a one-time industry in the city, which was brought here by the German settlers. They brought the practice of stuffing or "noodling" geese from Germany in the 1850s. Geese would be penned off and force-fed thick, doughy noodles several times a day. The geese would drink more water to help in digestion and this would cause the size of the liver to increase. The livers were then cut out when the geese were sent to market and the livers would be shipped to restaurants as far away as New York where "Watertown Stuffed Geese" on the menu signified freshness and excellence.

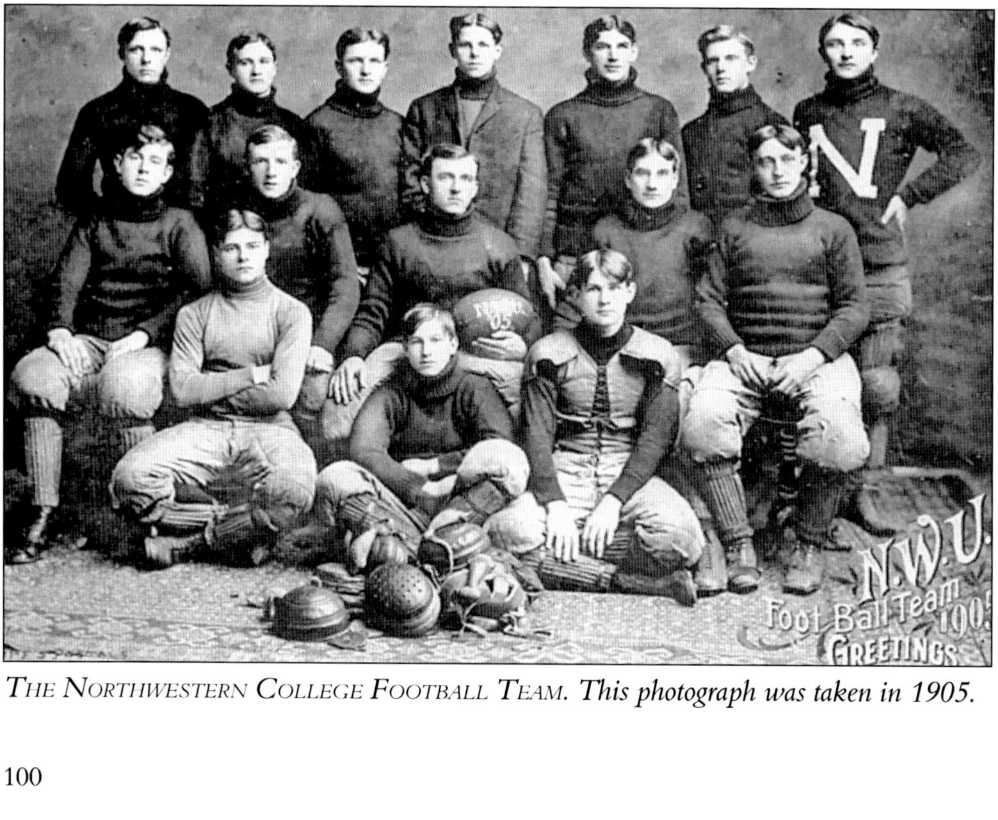

THE NORTHWESTERN COLLEGE FOOTBALL TEAM. This photograph was taken in 1905.

HARVEST JUBILEE AND CARNIVAL AD. This ad was for the 1899 carnival.

These livers were made into paté, which was considered a delicacy. Though never a major industry, the unique practice made a name for the city.

The stuffed geese industry experienced a gradual decline as the twentieth century wore on. The last time geese were noodled in the city was in the early 1970s when the Fred Rumler family produced the last genuine Watertown stuffed geese.

Lest the reader think that a gosling is a little ball of fluffy white feathers and therefore not to be feared, you would do well to remember that geese have a row of needle-sharp teeth lining their beaks and they are tenacious and fearless birds. The Watertown Gosling teams have gone on to win many state championships, pennants, and trophies for excellence in sports.

The *Watertown Daily Times* entered the scene on November 23, 1895, and soon became the leading newspaper in the city. It joined the ranks of other established newspapers of the time such as the *Watertown Gazette*, founded in 1879, the *Watertown Republican*, founded in 1860, and the German-language newspaper the *Watertown Weltburger*, founded in 1858. Other newspapers would come and go, but by the end of the 1930s, the *Daily Times* would become the only paper in Watertown, a position it maintains to this day.

The end of the nineteenth century in Watertown was marked by a grand Harvest Jubilee and Carnival held on September 13, 14, and 15, 1899. The celebration drew thousands into the city, which was decked out in all its finery. A grand parade with "allegorical floats" and carriages festooned with flowers, ridden in by prominent citizens, was the highlight of the event. In the words of the official souvenir program:

> The event shall truly be a Harvest Jubilee in every sense of the term, and Watertown will welcome her honored guests with that open-hearted hospitality for which she has long enjoyed a wide reputation. We are privileged to say that absolute freedom and generous amusement will be accorded the stranger within our gates, and we think that no one shall have cause to complain of the treatment accorded, or regret that a visit was paid to Watertown's first annual Harvest Jubilee and Carnival.

Thus, the nineteenth century drew to a close. The first 53 years of the city's history saw much upheaval and hardships. But Watertown, through it all, managed to survive and grow. And it would continue to prosper in the coming century.

FLORAL WAGON. This 1899 photograph shows the Woodard family in front of their North Washington Street home during the Harvest Jubilee and Carnival Parade.

8. The New Century Begins: 1900–1920

No matter where we have been since leaving here, there is but one place that [we] will always be welcome with the ardor that moves the heart and that is dear old Watertown. . . . there is no town anywhere whose people are more hospitable than the people of Watertown. . . . Watertown has contributed liberally to the commercial and industrial upbuilding and progress of Wisconsin and other states and she will continue to do so for here the man of the future is taught those lessons of thrift, honesty and industry which makes for good citizenship.

E.A. Kehr, Address at the First Home Coming Celebration
Watertown Republican, August 19, 1903

The new century began in Watertown with a fanfare of horns at midnight from the steeple of the Moravian Church. Throughout the city at balls or at private homes, people toasted the New Year, never realizing that the coming years would bring changes unlike any previously seen. One wonders what the early settlers would have made of the new surroundings, but most of the founding fathers had by this time either died or would pass away within the first ten years of the new century.

The era of the horse-drawn wagon was rapidly drawing to a close with the arrival on the city streets of the automobile. It is hard to imagine just what an impact cars made on life and on commerce. Autos brought about the creation of better paved highways and better marked thoroughfares and the auto allowed people to move further outside the center of the city, thus helping to create the concept of the suburbs. Just who was responsible for bringing the first automobile to Watertown is unknown, but by the early 1900s, they were being seen on the streets with increasing frequency. Despite the automobile's arrival, horse-drawn conveyances would still be seen on the streets of the city as late as the 1930s.

Actually, horseless carriages were seen in Watertown as early as 1878 when a race was held featuring steam-powered cars. This race began in Green Bay and ended in Madison with contestants traveling through Watertown on their way towards the finish line. A newspaper account stated that the people in Watertown were afraid of the steam machines. It went on to say that "they stood with eyes,

FIRST TROLLEY. This photograph shows the fanfare that welcomed the arrival of the first streetcar in Watertown on July 30, 1908.

ears, and mouths open, wondering where such a hideous-looking arrangement hailed from."

In 1912, the G.H. Hafemeister Motor Company was organized in Watertown to manufacture cars, but this appears to have been a very short-lived concern and it is unknown if any cars actually were made in the city.

In addition to autos, Watertown also received another form of mass transit heretofore not seen in the city, a trolley line. The line ran between Watertown and Waukesha and had been in the planning stage for over five years before it became a reality. On July 30, 1908, the first interurban trolley car, owned by the Milwaukee Electric Railway and Light Company (TMER&L) arrived in the city, amidst cheering throngs of people and a clamor of bells and whistles. Henry Bence was the motorman and Bert Olson was the conductor. The first paying passenger was Charles Gillis.

The early days of the trolley were not without a certain amount of danger. One of the first traffic fatalities in the area happened on July 25, 1912 when Watertown resident Emil Behl was killed when his auto was struck by a trolley at the Ixonia station, south of the city. The *Watertown Gazette* also reported a case of a ride on the trolley that was fraught with danger of another kind on February 19, 1909:

Have you ever been on a Watertown trolley car? It is a fine craft, rocking along in fine style. If the swaying motion doesn't exactly lull one to a state of blissful unconsciousness, it will assuredly make him at times feel like taking a good snooze. They have several little conveniences too for the security and comfort of the sleepy or seasick passengers. The window sills particularly were devised especially for convenience in resting arms and elbows when it is impossible to sit up without something to hold onto or lean against. A young gentleman from the West-Side has it in for the trolley cars. He says but little about it himself, but a number of happy and joyous fellow passengers are telling. He got on one of the cars the other night, and the only unoccupied space being by the side of a pretty, well-dressed and refined-looking girl, he took the seat, although with apparent diffidence. The young woman's elbow was on the window next to him. She had found it necessary to brace against something, being evidently worn out with a round of strenuous shopping and the car was careening and plunging along like a merry-go-round. When the car bumped (and) passed one of the side streets the girl's arm slipped from the window, and in some inexplicable way on to the young man's shoulder. She was certainly sound asleep, he says, and he is equally certain, in his modest way, that she did not open her eyelids previous to this unfortunate accident. He being a young man of retiring

THE LYRIC MOVIE THEATER, 1908. This theater at 206 Main Street was originally called the Palace and was the first motion picture theater in Watertown.

> disposition and somewhat inclined to bashfulness in the presence of ladies, found himself in a delicate position. It was very evident to the other passengers that it was a serious problem. The perspiration starting from his forehead showed this, also the fixed and glassy way in which he gazed at the "Uneeda Beer" advertisement on the opposite side. Several acquaintances of his among the passengers were making unseemingly exhibitions of mirth over his unfortunate predicament. One man was trying to place a bet that he would stay to the end of the line and back again, unless the girl woke up, and each and every villain agreed that he would stay on the car as long as he did. He didn't know what to do. If he got up, the girl would wake and be embarrassed; if he stayed, those devils in the car would never let him hear the last of it. Just when he had given up all hope, the conductor shouted, "tickets," and the girl awoke with a start, shot one glance at the bashful young man, smiled happily and went to sleep again.

The trolley line proved to be successful, operating in the city for over 30 years. In 1927, the TMER&L Company spent a whopping $100,000 to erect a modern terminal and train building in Watertown. Unfortunately, by the 1930s, ridership began to decline and finally the trolley system ceased operations. The final run was held on January 31, 1940. Shortly thereafter, the tracks and overhead wires were removed.

To take the place of the trolley line, which had a regular route through the city and out to the fairgrounds during the annual run of the Inter-County Fair, a series of private cab companies provided service to those in need of a ride. The earliest was a jitney line operated by Murray Higgins in 1915. The trolley and cab service, which is currently run by the city, were outgrowths of the omnibus transit service provided by a number of Watertown firms in the latter half of the nineteenth century.

New forms of entertainment began to appear. Where once the citizens of Watertown may have attended a local concert or play, now they could be found frequenting movie theaters and enjoying the "flickers" that ran several times a day. Movies made their first appearance in the city in the late 1890s. Joseph Herro opened the first permanent theater for the exclusive showing of motion pictures in 1903. He called his nickelodeon the Palace and it has the distinction of being the third movie theater to open in Wisconsin. This venture proved to be so successful that a string of similar theaters began to spring up throughout the city, bearing such fanciful names as the Lyric, the Majestic, the Pantorium and the Victor. By 1940, there were only two movie theaters in the city, the Savoy on the west side of Watertown and the Classic on the east side. The Savoy opened in 1938 in the former Wiggenhorn Cigar Factory building and was in existence through the 1950s. Willis Norton opened the Classic and that has proved to be the most successful of the lot, lasting up till the present time. The Classic was renamed the Towne Cinema in 1972.

MRS. WALTER NACK, HER SON TOM, AND PET HORSE. This talented horse was purchased from the Seibel Brothers Circus. (Bernhard and Eleanore Schroeder collection.)

Motion pictures, for all their novelty, did not mean the death knell of live entertainment. Throughout the early days of the new century, Watertown was still considered a prime town for theatrical touring companies, Chautauquas, lecturers, concerts, and circuses. Actually, Watertown had its own circus, the Seibel Brothers Dog & Pony Show. Emil Seibel and his son Edward formed it in 1903. They used the term "brothers" since that was common circus parlance at the time.

Emil Seibel had over 25 trained ponies and 35 trained dogs, which could do the most amazing tricks, in addition to several trained mules and monkeys. The show traveled by rail throughout Wisconsin, Iowa, and Illinois and did a good business at first. It operated for several seasons under various names until 1916 when declining interest caused the show to disband. The animals were sold and thus ended Watertown's one and only circus.

A footnote to this story of the Seibel circus concerns itself with one of the trained horses. After the show folded and the horses were sold off, one of them was purchased by a local butcher named Water Nack. Nack, who would later become mayor of the city in the 1940s, bought the horse for his children. This horse had many talents, one of which was the ability to walk up stairs. This fact was not wasted on the Nack children who were itching to see the trick performed. So, one Sunday as the church service ended, the younger Nack boys and their cousins ran ahead of their elders and reached the Nack home first. They brought the horse into the house and watched with glee as it walked up the stairs to their parent's bedroom. Unfortunately, this horse could only walk up, it couldn't walk down. Try as they might, the boys couldn't get the horse to budge. So, when the elder Nacks arrived home they were confronted with the sight of a horse staring forlornly out of the bedroom window at them!

Besides these forms of entertainment, there was a movement on the part of the newly formed Watertown Outdoor Art Association and the agitation of several prominent ladies to establish a park department. Public parks were an unknown commodity in the 1800s. Sommergartens maintained sumptuous lawns, of course, and cemeteries were considered popular picnic spots. Watertown also had a picnic spot known as Richards's Grove, but this was private land. Tivoli Island was also private land. There was no public park system. With this civic group pushing the cause, the city acquired a tract of land on the east side of Watertown owned by Samuel Kussel and from this created Riverside Park, one of the oldest

KUSSEL ISLAND CAMPGROUNDS. This was the site of what later became Riverside Park, one of Watertown's loveliest public parks.

and loveliest of the more than ten parks maintained by the city today. In addition, the city also maintains a soccer field, baseball diamond, and volleyball and tennis courts. There are also two golf courses in Watertown. The older of the two is the Watertown Country Club, which opened in 1922, and it maintains a private golf course. The Windwood Country Club, opened in 1993, is a public golf course.

The years preceding World War I were marked with a seemingly unending series of fairs and celebrations, beginning in 1903. In that year, a group of Watertown ex-patriots met in Milwaukee to formulate plans for a grand reunion of former residents to be called the Home Coming Celebration. These annual events featured parades, carnivals, speeches, and other festivities. The Home Coming Celebrations were held each year until 1911 when declining interest caused the yearly event to be dropped.

In the midst of this, the Watertown Inter-County Fair Association was founded. They secured land on Utah Street, in the southern part of the city, and erected a fine fairground, complete with exhibition halls and a driving track and grandstand. These fairs were held the third week in September from 1904 to 1926. The association had the reputation of attracting the best fair entertainers and circus performers on the circuits. The highlight of the Inter-County Fair was the balloon ascension. Declining interest also spelled its eventual demise. In 1927, the fair buildings were split up and sold off and a car dealership and the Watertown National Guard Armory building, which was built in the 1950s, today occupy the area. Circuses that come through the city yearly still set up their tents in this area, however.

Riding on the crest of this seemingly endless round of fairs and fetes was the creation of the Watertown Public Library in 1903. The need for a public library had long been stressed. The first attempt at establishing a library was when the Young Men's Association (a forerunner of the YMCA) opened a public reading room in their meeting space above the Bank of Watertown building on Main and First Streets in 1857. This proved to be very successful, but was unfortunately short lived. A strawberry festival was held in the 1870s to raise funds for a library, but again nothing came of this. In 1896, a group of citizens put together a subscription library. For a yearly fee, one could check out books, but this system soon failed since it was only accessible by those with the cash, not the general public. It was not until 1900 and the timely assistance of two prominent women, Mrs. Sara Woodard and Mrs. George Lewis, that things really got underway.

The ladies arranged to have a play performed in the city to raise funds, but the production only netted them $60. The Wisconsin Free Library Commission then stepped in and offered to help begin a larger fund drive. It raised $2,000, not enough to start a really good library, but nevertheless a library opened in Watertown. At first, the headquarters of the Watertown Free Public Library was on the second floor of Clara Weiss's millinery shop and held 2,700 volumes. In 1905, the library board applied to the Carnegie Foundation for a grant to build a proper library, but they were refused. On their second try, however, they were awarded $20,000 and building began. The library was finished in 1907. With

LINCOLN SCHOOL IN 1910. This building burned to the ground in 1945 and was rebuilt and dedicated in 1949. It still serves as an elementary school.

the addition of a children's room and meeting hall in 1930, the library proved to be one of the most pleasing and important spots in the city. In 1984, a major renovation was undertaken that greatly added to the library's space, while still maintaining the original structure designed by the noted architectural firm of Claude and Starck.

The opening of the public library was a great boon to the public school system in Watertown, which had been undergoing some changes of its own. In 1909, the 100th anniversary of Abraham Lincoln's birth, Union School #2 was rebuilt, and the students and faculty asked the Watertown school board for permission to name the new school after the Great Emancipator. This was granted. But then, Union School #3 asked if they could name their school building as well. After some deliberation, it was decided to name this one after Stephen A. Douglas, whom Lincoln ran against in 1860. Not long after this, Union School #4 asked if they could be called Louisa May Alcott, after the author of *Little Women*, but this was refused by the board as being frivolous. Instead, they were given the name Webster, after Daniel Webster, the great orator.

Union School #1, located on East Main Street, had become the city's high school in 1897 and, for many years, there had been grumblings of over-crowding and lack of space in this building. In 1916, the school board and the city went forward and purchased land along South Eighth Street and soon began the erection of a three-story brick high school building. It was dedicated in 1917. This school, with various additions, served the city until 1994 as the high school. In 1994, a new state-of-the-art high school was erected in the northwestern part of the city. The former school became the home of the Watertown Health and Wellness Center and, in 2000, the 1916 section of the old high school building was demolished.

Watertown was on the move in the early half of the new century. A shoe factory, the Beals and Torrey Company, opened in 1904 in a large brick building on South Water and Milwaukee Streets. Shoe factories would flourish in the city for many years, the last one closing in 1968. Today, the former Beals and Torrey building is an apartment complex.

Other industries that opened at this time included the Ira L. Henry Box Factory on Elm Street. It opened in 1900. Cardboard boxes of all description are manufactured here. Though the original plant was destroyed by fire in 1945, a substantial brick factory rose up from the ashes and continues today.

Two other industrial firms are worthy of mention here, the Washington Cutlery Company and the Monarch Tractor Company. The Washington Cutlery Company, later known as the Village Blacksmith Folks, was formed in Milwaukee in 1893, but the firm relocated to Watertown in 1907. This company

MONARCH TRACTOR. These farm machines were manufactured in Watertown from 1913 to 1928. This example is being driven by Ed Samuelson. (Watertown Historical Society collection.)

was quite successful and, by the 1930s, it was producing a full line of cutlery and garden tools. Today, this concern is known as Fisher-Barton. The Monarch Tractor Company was formed in Watertown in about 1913, and when World War I broke out, the factory began to manufacture large "crawler" tractors for earth-moving and other large tasks. The Monarch Company took over the former Kunert Plant on South Second Street and lasted until 1928 when the Allis-Chalmers Corporation purchased the parent company and the factory left the city. The former Monarch Tractor buildings were then taken over by another metal fabricating concern that operated for many years in Watertown, the Otto Biefeld Company.

To care for the sick, a hospital began operation in 1909. Previously, a local doctor had, for a short time, run a private hospital in the 1890s and, as early as 1900, a small hospital was operating out of a building on South First Street. In 1909, Dr. Charles Habhegger and Dr. Thomas Shinnick acquired the Charles Schiffler home on East Main Street for use as a hospital. It had an operating room, x-ray room, and 16 beds. In 1913, Shinnick left Watertown and sold his interest in the hospital. In 1914, the Missionary Sisters, Servants of the Holy Ghost, a

ST. MARY'S HOSPITAL. This early 1940s photograph shows the hospital during its heyday. It was located on East Main Street and was managed by the Missionary Sisters, Servants of the Holy Cross.

Catholic religious order, acquired the facility. A bequest of $10,000 allowed the hospital to grow and expand and, in October 1918, the newly enlarged St. Mary's Hospital was opened. In 1937, an addition was built with 37 additional beds and the old Schiffler home was demolished.

The hospital was in transition in the mid-twentieth century. Fundraising efforts in the 1950s and 1960s helped to update the facility, but new technology was increasing with such rapidity that the old building, even with constant remodeling, couldn't keep pace. The Catholic Sisters at this time also professed a desire to sell the building; so, in 1961, the city of Watertown bought the former St. Mary's Hospital and plans got underway to build a new complex. In 1971, the present Watertown Memorial Hospital opened on Hospital Drive and it continues to serve the city and the surrounding areas today.

In 1903, a second care facility opened, this one designed to care for the mentally handicapped, in Watertown. Lutheran groups known as the Children's Friend Societies or Kindefreund Societies established a home for the mentally handicapped in a large brick building on Margaret Street in the northern part of the city. This was the beginning of Bethesda Lutheran Home, a nationally known care facility. The home was located in Watertown due to the large and strong Lutheran groups in the city and because of Watertown's strong German heritage. A further incentive was the donation of 20 acres of free land made available to the home.

However, Bethesda could not take advantage of the land at first and when the lease on the Margaret Street building was up, the home transferred its base of operations for a time to Milwaukee. In 1910, Bethesda returned to Watertown and began the erection of a campus in the southwestern part of the city. The home quickly grew in the next few decades. The Bethesda Home has provided high-quality education, training, and care in a religious atmosphere for mentally handicapped persons for much of the twentieth century. Today, Bethesda continues to provide this care as one of the charitable arms of the Lutheran Church.

But just as the first ten years of the new century brought many pleasant events, the next ten years would usher in a gradual dimming of optimism as Watertown and the nation were threatened with the twin specters of war and pestilence.

The first of several devastating fires that would plague the city throughout the twentieth century occurred on June 20, 1909 when the G.B. Lewis plant, located on South Water Street on the west side of the river, caught fire and burned to the ground in a spectacular blaze. The city fire departments were out in full force, but all their efforts were in vain. The plant had stood on this spot since 1863.

Following on the heels of this disaster came the great Cyclone of 1914, which struck the northwestern part of the city on June 24, 1914. Though the windstorm lasted but a few minutes, it left thousands of dollars worth of damage in its wake. There were only two other occasions that tornadoes struck the city and did damage, one in 1873 and the Palm Sunday tornado in 1964. The latter storm did no actual damage to the city proper, but instead wreaked havoc on residents along

LEAVING FOR WAR. This photograph shows the men of Watertown leaving for the European front on August 17, 1917.

Highway Y in the Town of Watertown.

And then came the worst calamity of them all: World War I. Like most citizens of the United States, Watertown residents read the daily reports of hostilities in Europe. But in a city that was composed of a population of nearly 90 percent German heritage, it can be surmised that Watertown citizens were even more keenly in tune with the goings on. Many residents still had friends and family living in Germany and were keeping in touch with them. German was still heard on street corners, in saloons, churches, and stores. One of the most widely read newspapers in the county was the German-language paper the *Watertown Weltburger* (*World Citizen*). Even some of the streets in Watertown bore German names, such as Berlin Avenue. In a show of unity, there was a mass meeting just before the United States got into the fray to prove that the Germans in Watertown were loyal to the country. Nevertheless, that did not stop the rumors of treason and spying and soon anyone speaking German was being viewed as a suspected "Hun," or a traitor to America.

As a result of anti-German feelings, the German language course was dropped in the high school and German ceased to be heard as often in public as it had been. Churches began to introduce English services and, by the mid-1930s, German was dropped in almost all churches in the city. Streets with German names were quickly changed, including the aforementioned Berlin Avenue, which was renamed East Main Street.

German foods became Americanized and thus sauerkraut became "liberty cabbage" and the like. Those immigrants who were not naturalized when they first came to the United States were forced to register with the local post office or police department as aliens and they were issued identity books, which resembled passports, that they had to show if requested. The author's great-grandmother, who immigrated from Germany with her husband and family in 1868 and settled in Watertown, was never naturalized since, being a woman, she fell under the naturalization of her husband, who himself was never naturalized. As a result, she was issued one of these alien cards. Judging from her photo, it is laughable to imagine that the country was in danger of being overthrown by this little, frail-looking old woman. But such was the tenor of the times. The German culture, which gave Watertown much of its unique character, was almost entirely obliterated and would never completely return, even after the unpleasantness of the war was over.

As in times past, the young men of Watertown were quick to volunteer their lives for the service of their country. Watertown men quickly formed a unit named after the famed German unit in the Civil War known as Company E. This company left Watertown for Camp Douglas, amidst a grand parade and many tearful good-byes from friends and family on August 17, 1917. The company remained there until September 25 when it was transferred to Waco, Texas. Here the company became known as Company C, 120th Machine Gun Battalion and then for the duration of the war it was known as Company D. The regiment left Texas on February 4, 1918 for Camp Merritt, New Jersey. They left for France shortly thereafter, arriving in Brest, France on March 4, 1918.

Upon their arrival, Company D left for the Alsace front and, on May 18, the company was ordered into the lines where they remained until May 29 and were then sent to the reserves at La Chappelle. An order came to have the company go again to the front. Here it remained until July when it was transferred by train to Chateau Thierry where the company met with their first major battle. After serving in various parts of France, the company wound up serving in action in the Argonne Forest from September 20 to November 11. On November 11, 1918, bugles sounded to cease firing and it was reported that the armistice was signed. The *Watertown Daily Times* had reported the armistice prematurely on November 7th and so the city was forced to celebrate the end of the war twice.

Meanwhile, Company D, made up of Watertown boys, was transferred to various points in Germany and France until they were able to board a ship for home. They landed in New York on May 13, 1919 and were sent to Camp Grant, Illinois where they were finally mustered out. The war veterans arrived back in Watertown on May 21, 1919, and the welcome they received was incredible. Everywhere women and men wept to see their loved ones return. On Main Street, the crowds became uncontrollable. Bands appeared and everyone marched and sang until long into the night.

Of the original company, four members lost their lives: Sergeant F.L. Pitterle (for whom a local VFW post is named), Benjamin Potter, Fred Bergman, and Luke B. Dunnigan. This would be the last war in which an entire company of local men could be tracked throughout the conflict. World War II and other wars that would occur saw the men and women of Watertown well represented, but most served in different branches of the service and in separate companies.

As if the war was not bad enough, Watertown, like most cities in the United States, also suffered through the great influenza epidemic of 1918. How it actually began is uncertain, but the earliest reports of Watertown cases would seem to point to soldiers stationed at Camp Grant, Illinois who had contracted the disease, possibly from soldiers returning from Europe. In Watertown, one of the first flu deaths was that of Art Rabenhorst. In October 1918, the epidemic had gotten so severe that public meetings were canceled and special masks were issued to anyone going out and about in public. By the end of October, there were 94 confirmed cases of the flu in the city. Movie theaters and schools were closed. By November, an additional 58 flu cases were documented in just two days. All throughout the month, the cases of influenza seemed to fluctuate. Relief did not arrive until late in December.

By January 1919, Dr. C.J. Habhegger, a local physician, reported to the *Watertown Daily Times* that, "In spite of the new cases there was no need for panic as this disease gave proof of having run its course and was gradually dying out." Yet, deaths still occurred and would continue through the early months of 1919. And then the epidemic, for all intents and purposes, ended in Watertown.

Shakespeare wrote, "Oh brave, new world," and the men who returned from war would soon find out just how different this new world was from the one they had left just a few years earlier.

AUGUST *17, 1917. This crowd at the Watertown train depot was seeing the men off to war.*

9. Good Times and Bad Times: 1920–1940

Let us dedicate ourselves to the task of building a greater and better Watertown, thus contributing our share to the work of the pioneers and the men and women of the past 100 years in making Watertown a city we can all be proud of. In celebrating the centennial let us not forget the achievements of the past and let us not be insensible to the sacrifices which the pioneers of this section made so that we might have a modern city to enjoy.

Mayor R.W. Lueck, *Watertown Daily Times*, July 2, 1936

With the end of hostilities in Europe in 1918, the entire country began to return to normal. Life began anew, but with some changes on the horizons, most notably Prohibition. Brewing had been a major industry in the city since 1846 and, with the prohibition of the making and selling of intoxicating beverages, this meant that a major industry had to close down. It is to Watertown's credit that it never hitched its collective wagon to one industry so the city's economy was little affected by this sudden change. But the people of the city felt the effects of no beer and they began to react.

There was a rash of bootlegging or illegal manufacturing of liquor in the 1920s, which would not cease until the mid-1930s. In Watertown, an enterprising team of brothers named Ryan opened an illegal brewery on North Montgomery Street, which lasted for a good many years in the city since the brewery's best customer, according to legend, was the chief of police. Taverns closed and in their place ice cream parlors opened. The Hartig Brewery, the last major brewery in the city, shifted its operations from the making of beer to the making of ice cream and continued to prosper throughout the 1920s, with the slogan "Eat Hartig's Ice cream—It's Brain Food!"

Young men and women who had previously lived on farms began to abandon them in order to live and work in the city and take advantage of services, such as modern plumbing and electricity. New factories opened and found willing workers.

In 1920, in order to better promote the city, the Watertown Chamber of Commerce was founded to encourage industry and businesses to locate here.

The economy of the city and buying power of its inhabitants began to rise. Main Street, the business district of the city, entered its Golden Era.

New shops began to open, such as a branch of the J.C. Penney Store on Main Street in 1915, and Sears, Roebuck and Company on South Third Street. Older established business houses, such as Kusel Hardware, Watertown's pioneer hardware store that had opened in 1849; Schempf Brothers Big Cash Store; Keck Furniture, which opened in 1853 and is reportedly the oldest furniture store in Wisconsin; Salick's Jewelry Store, founded in 1853; and Fischer's Department Store, which was founded in 1895, still led the way and held their prominence. However, new shops, such as Woolworth's Five and Dime Store, which opened in Watertown in 1922, and much later the S.S. Kresge Dime Store would give them a run for their money.

It must have been a pleasure to go down Main Street at this time. One could sample the wares of at least seven bakeries (Koser's, Pagel's, Leopold's, the Sally Ann Bake Shop, the East Side Bakery, the Quality Bake Shop, and Stupka's), many of which would last into the 1980s; one could also stop in at Baumann's Candy Kitchen, the Classic Sweet Shop or have a Cream Jumbo candy bar, made by the Howard Candy Company of Watertown. If one was not in the mood for sweets or baked goods, there were also many meat markets located in the city, such as Nack's, Fendt's, or Bayer's, to name a few. Then there were millinery shops, such as Clara Weiss's, who would close her doors after a long time in business in the late 1920s, or men's clothing stores, such as Faber's Men Shop or Hertel and

MAIN STREET. This photograph of Watertown's Main Street was taken c. 1925. (Edward Stuebe collection.)

WILLIAM MCBOYLE'S AIRPLANE. This c. 1926 photograph was taken at the Inter-County Fairgrounds. (Arline Hildebrandt collection.)

Hoffmann. Ruesch's, Meyer's, and Spohn's were among the leading shoe stores. And if you needed something for the farm, there was the Charles Piper Leather Company or John Gessert's, which catered to the needs of the farmer, or Kramp's and the James Casey Company, which bridged the gap between the nineteenth and twentieth century by maintaining a blacksmith business while also selling cars.

There were numerous grocery stores during this time. This was the era of the so-called "mom and pop" corner groceries and just about every major thoroughfare had at least one such store, many operating through the 1960s. The merchants of the city would enjoy a long period of prosperity that would last until the 1970s and the arrival of large chain stores.

The city underwent changes as well and several improvements were made during this time. Arc lights, for example, were placed at Riverside Park in 1920, which allowed for nighttime baseball games. The old high school building on East Main Street, vacant since 1917 when the "new" high school on Eighth Street was built, was taken over by the city and used as an armory. The fire and police departments began to improve their methods of protecting the city and to bring modern methods into everyday use.

The bridge on East Main Street, known as Memorial Bridge, was rebuilt in 1923. Another set of bridge projects during the 1920s would create a major headache for the city council, thanks in large part to a firebrand mayor at the time, Dr. A.H. Hartwig. Dr. Hartwig was a member of a pioneer family and was a prominent and popular veterinarian. He was elected mayor in 1928. His term was relatively unremarkable until the city was made the beneficiary of a sizable amount of money from the estate of the late John W. Cole, a pioneer settler.

In his will, Cole left a certain amount of money to the city for various improvement projects, among them the establishment of a home for the elderly and a racing track. After many years of litigation between heirs of the estate and the city, the will was settled and money was made available through the sale of Cole properties in Watertown and in nearby Marshall, Wisconsin.

About this time, the Main Street bridge and North Fourth Street bridge both were in need of repair. Simply put, the city council wanted to rebuild the Main Street bridge using money from the Cole estate and make it a lasting memorial to him. The council also planned to issue bonds to help pay for the North Fourth Street bridge and to help defray any extra costs in rebuilding the Main Street bridge. Mayor Hartwig, remembering only too well the problems Watertown had had in the past with bonds, was dead set against this notion and he vetoed every resolution that called for the raising of bonds that came before him. Hartwig's plan called for the Cole money to be used to rebuild the Fourth Street bridge and any money left over to be used to repair the Main Street bridge.

In hindsight, this all seems very silly now and it is hard to imagine that this issue divided the city and caused great upheavals in city government throughout the remainder of the 1920s, but that is the way things went at this time—at least in Watertown. Ultimately, the Main Street bridge was rebuilt using money from the Cole estate in 1931 and with the election of a new mayor, Charles Lutovsky, in 1930, a relative calm was restored to the city council chambers. By this time, there would be no worrying about repairing or rebuilding bridges. The Great Depression was here and there were more important things to be concerned with. As for Hartwig, he would be re-elected mayor in 1934 and he died in office in 1936, a fighter till the end.

Changes in transportation were noticeable as well. In 1928, the beginnings of the Watertown Municipal Airport would be founded west of the city along Highway 19 by the Watertown Aero Club. Watertown citizens had been fascinated by air travel since aviator Farnum Fish made an appearance in the city in the early 1910s. Charles Lindbergh, fresh from his solo flight across the sea, flew over the city in 1927 and, in the mid-1920s, William McBoyle was giving paying customers thrill rides by taking them aloft in his bi-plane. The Watertown Municipal Airport would move to its present location, south of the city on what is now known as Airport Road, by the 1940s.

Auto use was on the rise. With the increase in the use of cars came the need for parking, which is still a hot issue in the city. In 1921, the enterprising Herro brothers opened one of, if not the very, first parking lots on Madison Street. They also ran a filling station in conjunction with their parking lot. Tourist camps, the forerunners of motels, began to open, one of the first being the Shady Nook on Highway 19 west of the city. Improved and better marked highways began to be created and the earliest one-way street in Watertown was established to better control traffic patterns. This street, created in 1921, was located within Riverside Park. And that was just the beginning! Stop-and-go lights soon followed, the first in Watertown being placed at the intersection of Third and Main Streets in 1925.

Several major fires took place in the 1920s, the most notable being the Turner Hall fire in 1928. This fire, of unknown origin, destroyed what was considered to have been Watertown's oldest public building. The heat from the fire was so intense that its radiance could be felt for blocks around. The National Guard had been using the hall for storage of its ammo and when the fire hit it, the building literally exploded. A new structure, still in use today, was built and dedicated on the site of the old hall in 1929.

But what of the people? In the 1920s, the citizens of Watertown were enjoying all the same sorts of things that everybody enjoyed. They attended circuses, for Watertown was still considered a prime stopover for circuses like Ringling Brothers, and they attended the movies. The first talking picture, *The Trial of Mary Dugan*, premiered at the Classic Movie Theater on East Main Street in 1929. Residents enjoyed attending the annual Chautauquas that would arrive each summer, as well as the occasional Methodist revival meeting. But the true pleasure spot of the city for many years, Tivoli Island, would not be available for Sunday picnics as of old, for after passing through several different owners it had, in 1921, been turned into a "first class chicken and duck farm."

AFTER THE FIRE. This photograph shows the ruins of the decimated Turner Hall following the March 8, 1928 fire.

Short skirts and rolled stockings began to be seen more often on the streets of the city, and many remarks were made about the indecent "baby vamps" who paraded about town with painted knees. A satirical poem regarding Watertown's problem with these young girls appeared in the *Milwaukee Journal* on August 25, 1921:

Watertown.
We have a swarm of baby vamps,
With their bobbed hair a-flying,
Who park beneath the Main street lamps
And send all the men a-shying.
They are the sirens of the town
In, oh! such shocking dresses;
The men all keep their eyes cast down
For fear of flying tresses.
Men crowd the streets to talk it o'er,
In groups for best protection;
And huddle closer, more and more,
At glances cast in their direction.
We're sorry for these helpless men
And look with understanding
Upon the words from mouth or pen
About the vamps disbanding.

Ministers predicted a bad end for these devotees of "flaming youth." One of the earliest cries of "there's nothing to do in this town," a plaintive cry still heard in the city, was also heard for the first time in 1921 in a letter to the editor of the *Watertown Daily Times*.

City parks were continuing to be developed in the 1920s with Memorial Park, the newest, making its debut in 1925. This park was located on the site of the former Fuermann Brewery on Jones Street. The actual development started in about 1914 but would not be finished until the late 1920s. Nevertheless, Memorial Park soon became a popular spot despite its being built on the shaky foundations of old brewery vaults, which caused sections of the park to sink throughout the 1930s. The park was in existence until the mid-1960s when it was sacrificed for the site of the current Municipal Building.

Washington Park, formerly Richards's Picnic Grounds and later a bicycle driving park, was purchased by the Watertown School Board during the 1920s for a playing field. This would be the scene of Watertown High School's many football and baseball games until 1994 when a new high school and playing field was erected north of the city.

In the wintertime, Watertown came alive with numerous skating clubs, such as the Gondolier and Silver Creek Skating Clubs. There was also ice boating on the river. At one point, an enterprising fellow adapted an airplane propeller, placed it on the back of an ice boat, and nearly blew the clothes off his fellow club members as the boat took off like a shot.

Sledding and skiing were also popular and the best place for these sports in Watertown was located on Richards Hill, near the famed Octagon House Museum, then still a private home. William Thomas, grandson of John Richards and himself a quirky sort of fellow, erected a large ski slide on the south side of the house, along what is today Charles Street in the southeastern section of the city. From this slide, one could, if the wind was at your back, slide down the chute and sail clear across the frozen Rock River and end up on the east side of the river. This was a popular spot on winter afternoons until one terrible day in 1924 when two brothers, Hubert and Leonard Born, decided to slide down the hill at nightfall. Normally, there was a look-out placed at the base of the hill along Concord Avenue to watch for passing cars and wagons, but since this was at night, there was no one to watch for the traffic. As the boys came down the hill, they were struck by a horse-drawn cutter and after lingering for a day, they both died. Since then, it has been illegal to slide down Richards Hill.

And yet for all of the advances of the era, there were still reminders of the city's pioneer past. In January 1921, for example, a pack of timber wolves, once a

BABY VAMPS. These young women were photographed on Main Street in the 1920s. (Watertown Historical Society collection.)

scourge of the pioneer settlers, was discovered roaming the area near the city. The past has never been far removed from the present in Watertown.

On October 24, 1929, the nation's bubble burst with the collapse of the stock market. The ramifications of this event would not be truly felt in Watertown until 1931, however, when the first relief program was established. The Great Depression would rage on in the city as it did elsewhere throughout the nation, though its effects, at least outwardly, would not be noticed in the city at first. This may be due to the nature of the citizens, many of whom were raised in an atmosphere of thrift.

These sons and daughters of German and Irish settlers not only knew how to live within their means, but they also knew how important it was to care for their neighbors. Thus, where in other cities the poor were out on the city streets begging, in Watertown there were no such occurrences, though that is not say that there weren't homeless people in the city. So-called "tramps" or transients would often come through the city looking for handouts and had been doing so since the mid-1800s. In the 1930s, many of these men would come into the public library to get warm and sleep, or they would arrange to be arrested and thus have a warm room and a meal. But these were exceptions rather than the rule.

It is a remarkable testament to the citizens of Watertown that, though they had to make clothing last and many didn't eat well and often retired hungry each night, no one ever went entirely without. The churches saw to the administering of funds. A notable example occurred in 1933 when the choir of Saint Mark's Lutheran Church decided to use the music funds they had saved to buy Christmas candy for the children of the Sunday school as a holiday treat.

The Watertown public schools implemented hot lunch programs in the 1930s to ensure that students got a hot meal at least once a day. People began to raise crops in their gardens, and the barter system (never truly a thing of the past in the city) was used for the purchase of meat and as payment for services rendered.

In 1933, things began to get truly desperate. At this time, the dairy farmers of Wisconsin, agitated by Walter Sigler, began to stage a series of "milk strikes" to combat the low prices being paid for raw milk. In Watertown, which has always lain in the heart of dairy country, there were blockades and threats made against anyone trying to transport milk. In other areas of the state, the strike took a more violent turn, with bombs being placed in dairies. It took over a year before things settled down.

At the same time, newly elected President of the United States Franklin D. Roosevelt declared a series of "bank holidays" and closed several banks across the United States. The effect of this action in some places was catastrophic, but in Watertown, the residents showed little concern. Banks in Watertown have always, throughout many depressions, recessions, and "panics," remained strong and sound. And so it was that after the banks opened again, Watertown's financial institutions were all found to be on sound footing. This did not stop many people in Watertown from hoarding money in their homes, however.

EDWIN WITTE. Witte, a Watertown native, created the national Social Security Act.

The government created several "make work" job programs during the 1930s and in Watertown some of these included the landscaping and development of city parks, street repair work, the erection of a new sewage disposal plant in 1932, and the building of the municipal swimming pool, which was completed in 1942.

In 1933, President Roosevelt repealed the Prohibition Act and Americans could once again indulge in their favorite pastime of enjoying a night out without the threat of being arrested. According to a report in the *Watertown Daily Times*, there were tears in many an old-timer's eye when the big whistle on the Hartig Brewery blew again to signal workers to their jobs. The Hartig plant ceased making ice cream and went into the manufacturing of beer in full force, but things would never be the same and the company continued its gradual decline, leading ultimately to bankruptcy and its eventual closing in 1947.

In 1935, in an effort to stem the effects of the Depression on United States citizens, Roosevelt passed the Social Security Act. Edwin Witte, who grew up in the Town of Watertown, developed the act. By the end of the 1930s, the economy began to look better and, in the words of President Roosevelt, "Prosperity was right around the corner."

SCHEMPF BROTHERS DEPARTMENT STORE, 1935. Its closing in 1936 brought an end to the most successful and one of the oldest department stores in the city. (Herman and Mary Rohr collection.)

Main Street businesses underwent changes during this time as a result of the Depression. Small grocery stores banded together to form the "Selrite Stores," a sort of co-operative marketing effort in which each shopkeeper helped the other. Main Street's oldest department store, Schempf Brothers, closed in 1936, bringing to an end a business that had been part of the city since 1848. When the Schempf Brothers store shut its doors, the building was divided into two separate stores, Montgomery Ward and the S.S. Kresge Company. Montgomery Ward would remain on Main Street until the late 1950s and when they left, the Kresge Company took over the entire building.

Nonetheless, it was not all gloom and doom during this period. In 1935, for example, Watertown made headlines when the *Milwaukee Journal* broke the story of Arthur "Turkey" Gehrke, a local saloonkeeper. He was normal in every way except for the fact that he spent each winter in bed. As a younger man, he experienced stomach pains and, being morbidly afraid of doctors, tried all sorts of home remedies. One of the most effective combatants against his supposed pains was complete bed rest. Since these pains seem to come on him at the onset of winter, Turkey decided to take to his bed each year at the start of the winter season and not rise until the signs of spring.

Watertown people were used to eccentric characters, such as Bill Cody, the son of early physician Dr. James Cody, who was himself an eccentric. Bill Cody was once hauled before the court in a sanity hearing and found to be in full control of his mental faculties. Every time thereafter, when he was in an argument with someone and they would say, "You're crazy!" he would remark, "No I'm not, and I have the court papers to prove it!" Oh yes, eccentric people were not news to people in Watertown and so they didn't make much of a fuss about Turkey's sleeping habits. But to an outsider, this was big news.

Turkey, who got his name when a little boy tried to say "Gehrke" and it came out sounding like "Turkey," soon found himself the object of media attention. Reporters from all over the United States began to descend upon him, asking him about his sleeping habits, etc. He went to New York with a local bowling team, was featured on the "Ripley's Believe It or Not" radio program, and was even interviewed by the BBC in London. Turkey milked the publicity for all it was worth and he was known to the world as "The Human Hibernator." He traded on his popularity for many years, finally succumbing to health problems stemming from complications of anemia in 1942.

In 1936, Watertown marked a milestone. The city held a grand celebration of the 100th anniversary of its founding. The event was marked with a year-long series of historical events, a grand parade, and the publication of a little historical booklet. The queen of the festival should have been Mrs. Anna (Richards)

ARTHUR "TURKEY" GEHRKE AND HIS WIFE, GRACE. Turkey Gehrke was known as the "Human Hibernator." (Jim Tobalske collection.)

Thomas, the daughter of John Richards, but she died early in 1936, so that title went instead to Mrs. Netta Holmes, a granddaughter of Timothy Johnson. The Watertown Historical Society, which was founded in 1933, began to make itself known and, in 1937, it would inherit the famed Richards mansion, today known as the Octagon House, which it runs as a public museum.

Also in 1936, culture in Watertown received a shot in the arm with the founding of the Curtain Club, a community theater company. Upholding a tradition that goes back to the Watertown Dramatic Association of the 1860s and the Concordia Musical Society, this new theater company began a career that would span over 39 years and bring many plays to the theater-going public in Watertown.

Watertown, by the end of the 1930s, was beginning to shake off the more devastating effects of the Depression, only to be plunged headlong with the rest of the United States into World War II.

MRS. SHELDON E. (NETTA CHADWICK) HOLMES. Mrs. Holmes was queen of the 1936 Centennial Parade. She was the granddaughter of Timothy Johnson, the founder of Watertown.

10. The War Years and Beyond: 1940–1960

"Watertown remains gloriously obstinate", remarked Frank C. Blied, Madison, President of the National Turnerverein. "It refuses to yield to every whim and fashion. So long as Northwestern College continues to teach the beauty of the German language and the citizens there and round about have respect for the ideals of the pioneers; so long as housewives feed their families good wholesome German cooking; and the name of Carl Schurz, who lived there, is revered as a great German-American, Watertown will be distinctive."

Fred L. Holmes, *Old World Wisconsin, Around Europe in the Badger State*

In 1939, the specter of war again began to loom ominously over Europe and the world with the rise of Adolf Hitler and the Nazi Party in Germany. The United States would not actually get involved until the destruction of Pearl Harbor in 1941 by the Japanese, but already in October 1940 the first troop of men from Watertown left for army training. That would be just the beginning.

The men from Watertown joined all the various branches of the armed forces, but in the early days of the war, one troop that was made up of mostly Watertown volunteers was Battery F of the 126th Field Artillery. This troop left Watertown on October 22, 1940 for Camp Beauregard, located in Alexandria, Georgia. Later this company moved to Camp Livingston, Louisiana where the regiment was divided into the 126th and 173rd Field Artillery Battalions. The 126th, with 105 Howitzer guns, served in the Pacific area, and the 173rd, with 155 "Long Tom" guns, served in the European theater of operations.

Of the men and women who served, 32 never returned. Those who lost their lives for their country were Clarence Dittman, Wallace West, Paul Bittner, Leslie Schoechert, Howard Steckling, Leland Newcomb, Elroy Gebhardt, Oscar Backhaus, Dennis Cowan, David Draeger, Raymond Friewald, Robert Hayhurst, Robert Koehler (the third soldier in the city to die; a VFW post is named for him), Russell Beaudoin (the second casualty of the war; a VFW post is named for him as well), Vernon Copsey, Edwin Wendt, Victor Schultz, Ralph Burdick, Lyle Altwies, Robert Kuenzi, Kurt Schmeling, Clarence Zautner, Gilbert Jansa, Richard Barnes, Harlyn Schroeder, Thomas Nickels, Lloyd Kuehl, George

THE DRAFT. These Watertown men were photographed in front of the Selective Service Bureau on East Main Street.

Thompson, George Shepard (reportedly the first from Watertown to die; he died while on furlough in the city), Harry Schultz, Lester Lange, and John Pritzlaff.

On the homefront, life during the war was marked with rationing and shortages. Meat and rubber were in short supply, as were nylon stockings and chocolate to name but a few of the things average Americans could not get in large supply. Ration books and stamps were issued for foodstuffs, gasoline, and oil. Blackouts were instituted, with the first being held in Watertown on December 10, 1942. Air raid wardens patrolled the neighborhoods making certain that everyone obeyed the blackout orders. In 1942, Walter Nuremberg, a longtime member of the city council, requested that the United States War Department send the city an anti-aircraft gun for its protection. The request was denied. However, in 1944, the city did receive a shipment of gas masks and helmets.

Factories began to manufacture materials for the war, such as propellers and metal housings. The Waukesha Foundry, located in Watertown, was awarded the prestigious "E" award for their efforts on behalf of the war. Women began to take over jobs once exclusively the province of men. Migrant workers also made their appearance in the city, starting in 1943 when the Watertown Canning Company, founded in 1912, brought a crew of Jamaican workers to help gather crops in their fields. In 1944, German POWs also began to start working for the Canning Company. These prisoners were brought in from camps in the area, such as the POW camp in nearby Waterloo and the one at the County Fairgrounds in Jefferson.

On Main Street, things were humming right along. The major change was in the city's shopping habits. In January 1944, the city decided to make Friday nights *the* night for shopping, rather than Saturday mornings, as had long been the tradition. This tradition continues up to the present time.

A rather unpleasant reminder of Watertown's former reputation as a rather disloyal city acquired during the Civil War resurfaced in 1944 when the infamous "Gentile League" was founded and began to make scandalous headlines. This small group of men and women had strong anti-Semitic views. They created enough noise to bring them to the attention of the state authorities who put them out of business later in the year. By the end of the 1940s, this group was but a memory.

In 1945, World War II came to an end and Watertown celebrated in high fashion. The men soon began returning and with their return, a new problem presented itself, a shortage of housing. In order to compensate for this, the city took over the old city circus grounds in the Fifth Ward and turned it into a Quonset hut village.

MAIN AND FIRST STREETS, 1944. This photograph shows the busy downtown shopping district at the close of World War II.

MAIN AND SECOND STREETS, 1945. Business picked up as new stores opened.

The idea was that these simple structures would allow soldiers and their families to live on their own while they saved up for new homes or until new homes were built. In 1951, the huts were torn down and the land reverted to a playground and public park today known as Lincoln Park. Several Quonset huts still exist in the city and surrounding countryside.

The remainder of the 1940s passed quietly as people struggled to get their lives back in track. New industries opened, such as the Syncromatic Corporation in 1945. This firm became Watertown Metal Products in 1966 and is still in business today. Other industries that began in the 1940s and 1950s included Johnson Controls in 1956, a Milwaukee gas specialty company; Durant Digital Instruments in 1957; Lindberg's in 1953 (originally known as Heavi Duty), which made industrial furnaces; Allard Express, a trucking firm which began in 1951; and the Jaye Company in 1953, which made styrofoam goods. Commenting in 1960, the *Watertown Daily Times* stated, "According to older residents of the community no decade in the history of Watertown has produced a greater industrial growth."

An inter-city bus line was started in 1946 and would be in operation until declining ridership caused the city to discontinue the service in 1994. A Greyhound Bus Line service began in the city in 1947 and the company would maintain service to the city for over 40 years, finally coming to an end in 1991.

The city experienced several devastating fires during the latter half of the 1940s. These included the Ira L. Henry Box Factory fire in 1945, the Lincoln Elementary

School fire in 1946, the destruction of the Fleischman Malting Company building in 1946, and finally the disastrous fire that burned out the Bittner and Tetzlaff drug store on the corner of Second and Main Streets in December 1946. In each case, however, though the structures were destroyed or seriously damaged, they were later rebuilt and business went on.

A footnote to the Lincoln School blaze concerns a young boy who heard about the fire. He ran all the way home to get his schoolbooks and raced back to the fire to toss them in. He thought he would never have to go to school again. Imagine his surprise when the next Monday he was back in school in a temporary location!

Perhaps the most significant change during this time period that would affect the city was in its governing. Prior to 1948, a duly elected mayor and board of aldermen governed Watertown. But in 1948, feeling that the city needed a change in the way it was being run, the public spoke and after the election of 1948, the city went under the council-manager system of government, with Dean Van Ness as the first city manager. Though strenuously objected to in many quarters, the city was governed under this system until 1960 when the mayor-alderman system was reinstated.

By the end of the 1940s, Watertown's population had risen to 11,301, an increase over 1930 when the population stood at 10,000. The 1950s and the so-called "baby boom" would cause the city's population to rise steadily.

THE IRA L. HENRY BOX COMPANY FIRE. This 1945 blaze lit up the night sky. (Watertown Historical Society collection.)

THE BITTNER & TEZTLAFF DRUG STORE FIRE. This 1946 photograph shows firefighters battling the blaze. (Watertown Historical Society collection.)

The 1950s began on an unpleasant note with the outbreak of a war, known euphemistically as a "conflict," in Korea. The Korean War began on June 15, 1950 and American participation in it ended on July 27, 1953. During that 37-month period more than 54,000 Americans died, including 8,390 from Wisconsin. Over 900 men from the Watertown area were drafted and served. Many never returned.

In 1952, "Operation Skywatch" began in the city. This program monitored the skies for enemy planes and also UFOs. There was a UFO scare in the area that following July. This all was an outgrowth of the Cold War and fear of Communists and atomic weapons. Civil defense shelters were built in schools and public buildings and bomb shelters made an appearance. People were uneasy and on edge. They needed something that would calm their minds and help keep them from worrying about things over which they had no control. In Watertown, that meant turning to radio and television.

On April 2, 1950, radio station WTTN 1580 AM, made its inaugural broadcast with these words, "This is Radio Station WTTN in Watertown located on the third floor of the Wisconsin National Bank Building, 104 West Main Street in Watertown." At last, the city had a means of on-the-spot reporting of the kind a newspaper couldn't provide. This prompted a "friendly" rivalry between the radio station and the *Watertown Daily Times* that lasted for many years. Albert Gale, Jack Yoe, and Carl Kolata, who later served as mayor of the city, founded WTTN Radio. Over the years, WTTN has undergone several format changes, from easy listening to country. Currently, its format is all talk radio.

As for television, reportedly one of the earliest TV sets ever seen in the city belonged to industrialist Richard Jaye who owned a set in the late 1940s. People came from all over to the Jaye home in order to experience this new medium. Shortly thereafter, Edward Stuebe opened the first TV repair service. By the end of the 1950s, TV antennas would dot the skyline of the city.

One other innovative trend in the entertainment field was the creation of the outdoor drive-in movie theater. Watertown people could travel to either Beaver Dam to the north or Jefferson to the south to see a drive-in movie and, for a short period of time, they also had the luxury of seeing a local drive-in located on Highway 19 west of the city. Movies were still a very popular form of entertainment and would remain so, despite the hypnotic pull of television.

The 1940s and 1950s were a popular time for dances. On any given Friday or Saturday night, one could find a dance being held at a local hall such as Turner Hall or the Elks Club. Throngs of people who came to dance and to be seen attended these events, and many romances began at a public dance. There were masked

CITY BUS. This Watertown city bus was photographed c. *1950.*

balls, cotillions, and dances held to commemorate every conceivable holiday. One needed little excuse to get together to "cut a rug" on the dance floor.

This was the heyday for Watertown orchestras and dance bands such as Babe Schoenath's Orchestra, Erline Gritzner and the Belles (an all-girl orchestra), Bob Strege and the Goosetown Dutchmen, and Red Doege and the Dizzy Sizzlers. Each band had a following and each had a specialty. The one thing these dance bands had in common was their ability to provide music for the dance-crazed Watertowners who wished to "trip the light fantastic." These bands were upholding a tradition that stretched back to the very earliest days of the city's history when musicians William Sacia and his brother Austin played for the very first Fourth of July celebration in Watertown in 1840 while the settlers danced through the night.

Another innovation at this time was the advent of fast food restaurants or "drive-ins." The earliest example of a drive-in restaurant was the Maple Leaf Barbeque, which was opened by Alton "Fats" Gritzner in about 1934. His stand was located on South Third Street and he specialized in hot beef sandwiches with a special homemade relish. This stand operated into the late 1960s. Following on the heels of this was an A&W Root Beer stand, which opened on River Drive in the early 1940s. Other drive-ins included the Tip Up on Highway 16, which opened in 1961; Schuett's on Main Street, which opened in 1955; the Tastee-Freeze on North Church Street, which opened in 1955; the Penguin on West Main Street, which opened in 1956; and the Dog N' Suds on Highway 26 north of the city, which opened in 1962.

Fast food in the modern sense of the word began in Watertown with the opening of a Mars Restaurant in 1969 on East Main Street. This restaurant soon

ERLINE GRITZNER AND THE BELLES. This was one of many dance bands and orchestras to come out of Watertown in the 1940s and 1950s. (Frank and Georgeanne Lindemann collection.)

THE TASTEE-FREEZE DRIVE-IN. This was one of many forerunners to the fast food restaurants of the present day that located in Watertown, (Watertown Historical Society collection.)

became Robbies and then the Red Barn before becoming an optometrist's office. Today, this site houses a Hardee's Restaurant. Other fast food places included a McDonald's, which opened on South Church Street in 1977. Today, several fast food restaurants serve the hungry citizens of Watertown.

Business began to experience a shift and, through the 1950s, new factories opened and long established stores either expanded or closed entirely. For example, in 1954, the very first supermarket, the National Tea Company store, opened on the site of the former Hartig Brewery on Cady Street. This signaled the death knell for corner grocery stores in the city and their numbers began a slow decline through the 1950s and 1960s. The last "mom and pop" grocery store, Boyum's on North Fourth Street, would close in the mid-1970s, bringing a part of Watertown's business history to a close.

The last millinery shop in Watertown, operated by Miss Cecilia Molzahn, closed in 1954 as well. Most people by this time now found it more convenient to go to department stores, such as Fischer's, Woolworth's, Kresge's, Sears, or Penney's, to do their shopping. Thus, the concept of one-stop shopping was born.

In education, the very first Joseph E. Davies scholarship was awarded in 1952 at the Watertown High School. Davies (1877–1958) was the son of a Welsh carriage maker and his wife was the first ordained female minister of the Gospel in Wisconsin. He was born in Watertown, went through the public school system,

THREE WATERTOWN MEN WHO MADE GOOD. Joseph E. Davies, ambassador to Russia under FDR, was photographed in 1937 with Ralph David Blumenfeld, editor of the London Daily Express, *and Leonard Broenimann, the "Flour King." (Watertown Historical Society collection.)*

and graduated from the University of Wisconsin with a degree in law. He became a practicing lawyer and ultimately this led to a political career. He attained the post of ambassador to Russia while serving under President Franklin D. Roosevelt and later wrote a best-selling book on his life in Russia entitled *Mission To Moscow*, which was made into a film starring Walter Huston. Davies retired from active service in the 1940s and in the 1950s, he decided to create the Davies Scholarship for academic excellence. The Davies Scholarship is given out at many schools in the area to this day and is considered a very prestigious honor.

The high-water mark of the 1950s came on June 27, 1954 when the city of Watertown held a grand celebration and parade to honor the 100th anniversary of the city's having been granted a city charter. The year-long festivities included beard-growing contests, contests to see who could create dresses of the period, a contest to pick the queen of the centennial, and a grand pageant depicting various scenes from Watertown's history and the first publication of a city history written by Marcella Killian, longtime secretary of the Watertown Historical Society.

The city came together to pay homage to its past and to celebrate life in a small Midwestern town.

Never mind that it was a year late.

CENTENNIAL PARADE, 1954. This photograph shows the Watertown Baton Corps.

11. A Time of Transition: 1960–1980

The East Side Bakery, Marge & Joe's World Bar, gas stations, the L&L Luncheonette, a large dandelioned field bordered by "the wall" where teenagers sit—these are the elements of Watertown's Main Street. The sidewalk is studded with cast iron planters, nine feet off the ground so children and animals won't tear out the petunias. And on the corner of Sixth and Main, a peculiarly America constellation: a green popcorn stand, a Bell Telephone booth, a mail box, and on the side of the Hotel Washington, a sign painted in red and yellow, "Chinese Food."

Lynn Eden, *Crisis in Watertown, The Polarization of an American Community*

The next two decades, the 1960s and 1970s, were turbulent times for the nation and Watertown was not immune from the upheaval as well. In fact, the 1960s began on a controversial note. It all began with a Department of Transportation decision to build a highway. This has always been a good way to create a battle in the city.

For many years, since the very beginning of the city in fact, the road leading out of Watertown to the south was through South Third Street. Traffic was heavy on this thoroughfare, as can be imagined, and since the 1920s, there had been a movement afoot to reroute the highway through some other part of the city. However, this was always met with strong opposition.

This issue came up again in 1959 when the Department of Transportation decided that it was time to create a central way into the city. They were planning on a major project of highway construction that would reroute Highway 26 south of the city and bring it into Watertown, where it would link up at South Church Street. When news of this plan was presented to the city, it created a storm of protest.

Tempers flared and even the clergy at Saint Bernard's Catholic Church got into the fray. No one wanted this quiet street to be upset and neighbors presented petitions against the building of the new road, but it was to no avail. By 1961, the highway was constructed, thus opening the way to new, untapped real estate for potential retail development. Within the next few years, this vacant land would become the biggest threat to Main Street's dominance as the commercial district of the city.

This new highway led to the construction of the Highway 16 bypass, located on the east side of the city. The bypass opened in October 1961. The day after it opened, the first accident occurred there and, in November 1961, the first traffic-related fatality took place on the newly opened road. The issue of bypasses for the city has been hotly debated since this time period. In 2002, it was decided to create a second bypass on the western side of Watertown.

Business continued to remain in a state of flux throughout the next few years. Merchants began to feel the loss of customers to large shopping centers in Madison and Milwaukee, so they began to offer special promotions that were aimed at keeping Watertown shoppers in Watertown. They began by creating a special sales event known as Maxwell Street Days, which proved to be so successful that it became a yearly event. The first Maxwell Street Days was held on July 20, 1960. Then, on May 19, 1965 the first "Moonlight Madness" sale event, where stores remained open later than their usual 9:00 closing time, took place. Maxwell Street Days still continues in Watertown, but since 2001, it has been known as the Main Street Splash and in addition to sales, dances and other events are offered in order to attract potential customers to downtown Watertown.

The author grew up during the 1960s and 1970s in Watertown and from a personal viewpoint, I can tell you that it was a wonderful time to be in the city.

THE FIRST MAXWELL STREET DAYS. This was Watertown in 1960. (Watertown Historical Society collection.)

Of course, I am looking at all of this from hindsight, but the shops seemed forever filled with people and the street was thronged with them. If the kind reader will indulge me, I will take you on a personal tour of Main Street at this time.

The city still had a bus service and it ran by my home on North Warren Street in the northwestern area of the city. On Friday night, for that was the night for shopping in those days, I would board the bus and it would transport my best friend and myself. We would alight at Main and First Streets and go to Drost's Smoke Shop first, always! They had the best selection of comic books and magazines and, in addition, they kept the girlie magazines in a locked glass case in the center of the store, which I always thought was mighty thoughtful of them.

From Drost's, we would wend our way up the street to the east to the first of our major shopping spots, Kresge's. As I close my eyes, I can still see and smell the place. Upon entering the first set of doors, one found themselves in the kitchenware and stationery department. Along the west wall was the pet department where one could buy goldfish or canaries. In the back, or south wall, was the furniture department. Turning to the east, almost in the center of the store, was heaven—two aisles of toys and the largest coloring book display in the city, I believe. The many hours spent in intense concentration and decision-making there are unfathomable.

DOWNTOWN SHOPPING DISTRICT. This photograph of Main and Fourth Streets in Watertown was taken c. *1961.*

ANOTHER VIEW OF DOWNTOWN, C. 1961. This photograph was taken at the intersection of Main and Second Streets.

On the eastern wall of the store was the lunch counter, which always seemed busy. It was hard to get two seats together. As a very young child, my father took me there for my first taste of a cherry Coke. The only other place that measured up to Kresge's was Woolworth's, usually our final destination of the evening.

Woolworth's in Watertown had three distinct ways to enter the store, near the lunch counter, near the sewing supplies on the corner of Main and Fourth Streets, or the fire entrance located off Fourth Street. We used every entry at one time or other.

Woolworth's was a place where you looked around, bought candy at the center counter display, looked at the pets department (goldfish, canaries, and the occasional box turtle or hamster), looked at the toy department, and then settled down to pool your money and buy a plate of french fries with your friend. Nearby were the comic books and Woolworth's had a rather good selection, as I recall.

By this time, it was nearly 8:30 and time to catch the bus for home. We would always get on in front of Kline's Department Store; that way, we could ride the long way home via the east side of the city, stopping at 9:00 in front of the Gas and Electric Company building on Third and Main, and then home. Main Street was in its silver period at this time. Little did anyone think that by the end of the 1970s, the focus of business would shift from Main Street to South Church Street.

In 1975, the Watertown branch of the F.W. Woolworth Company Five-and-Ten-Cent Store closed down, followed in 1983 by the closing of the S.S. Kresge Company Dime Store. But by this time, no one seemed to notice, since business patterns had shifted to the south of the city. This began with the opening of Shopko in 1968. Following Shopko came Value Village in the early 1970s, then Farm and Fleet. Longtime stores on Main Street began to drop out of sight, including the J.C. Penney store, which had been a fixture on Main Street since 1915. The Penney store left in the early 1980s and moved to a store south of town adjoining Shopko before leaving the city. Sears, a longtime downtown store, moved several times and finally left the city for a time, only to reestablish itself on Highway 26 south of the city in the late 1990s. Retail store spaces were rapidly being taken over by service industries, such as real estate agencies, investment firms, and insurance agencies.

Despite the many changes going on, the city continued to grow during the 1960s and 1970s. In 1964, the first dial telephone system in Watertown was

VALUE VILLAGE, 1971. This was one of the first retail shopping centers on South Church Street. (Watertown Historical Society collection.)

Watertown Municipal Building. This structure was erected on the site of Memorial Park and still serves the city as its city hall and police and fire departments.

introduced, with "261" being the first prefix. By 1978, increased population forced the telephone company to introduce a second prefix, "262." A third prefix, "206," was introduced in 1995.

A new municipal building was erected in 1965 on the site of the former Memorial Park on Jones Street. The former city hall on First Street, which had been built in 1885, was torn down to make way for a very picturesque parking lot. Watertown also acquired a new post office in 1962. The former post office building, built in 1912 on Second Street, was found to be too antiquated for modern usage, so the city purchased a lot on Dodge Street in the southern part of the city containing several lovely Victorian mansions, demolished them, and cleared the land. In 1962, the new post office was dedicated. As for the former post office building, it served as the headquarters for the local Moose Lodge until the early 1970s and, in 1972, it was demolished to create yet another charming lot for cars.

The 1960s were a time of building and, accordingly, new homes went up and new schools were built as well. Douglas School, which had been meeting in the old Union School building on Lincoln Street, moved into a new building on

Center Street in 1961 and, in 1967, Riverside Junior High School (now Middle School) was built on top of the former Lutovsky swamp on the east side of the city. Previously, the junior high school met in the Watertown High School building on Eighth Street. An indoor swimming pool was constructed as part of Riverside Junior High School in 1976 and this has proven to be a popular spot for those who like to swim during the winter and for swimming classes.

In addition to the public schools, a new college opened in 1977 when Madison Area Technical College opened a Watertown campus on the western extreme of the city limits. This tech school was an outgrowth of the vocational school system, which had been in place in the city since the 1930s.

In 1966, the first steps were taken to create a retirement and skilled care center for the growing number of senior citizens in Watertown and the surrounding area. Accordingly, land in the northern part of the city, formerly used as vineyards in the 1860s, was donated by Dr. Milton Ochs to the Western District of the Moravian Church, with the express purpose of building a senior citizens' home. This became Marquardt Memorial Manor. Construction began in 1967 and it was formally opened in 1969. Since that time, an entire village of retirement homes and assisted living apartment complexes has been built, all under the umbrella management of Marquardt Manor.

THE MALDANER MANSION. This was one of several large Victorian homes that were razed in order for the new post office to be built in 1962.

THE OLD POST OFFICE. Built in 1912, this edifice was turned over to the local Moose lodge after the new post office was built in 1962. It was used by the lodge until 1972 when it was torn down to make way for a charming parking lot. (Watertown Historical Society collection.)

Marquardt Manor is just one of several assisted living and low-income senior housing complexes in Watertown. Other facilities include Beverly Terrace, which began in 1972 as the Watertown Skilled Care Center; Johnson Arms, which opened in 1974 on North Water Street; and the granddaddy of them all, Saint Joseph's Home for the Aged, which was opened by the Catholic Sisters of Charity in 1942 on Clyman Street. Sadly, Saint Joseph's closed in 1998.

The Vietnam War was an ominous specter that loomed over the United States during the 1960s and 1970s. Over 350 men from Watertown served in the war, which lasted from December 22, 1961 to May 7, 1975. There were five men from Watertown who lost their lives in this war. Those who died in the service of their country were Michael Bartelme, Ralph L. Blauvelt, Dale Schwefel, Ronald D. Shephard, and Michael J. Wagner.

In Watertown, as in other places, there were some signs of discontent with the established way of doing things and with the war in Vietnam. The local National Guard unit in the city, which had been formed in 1920, was sent to Madison during the bombings of the University of Wisconsin Science Building during the 1970s. But for the most part, things were quiet here. Until 1967. In that year, a minister named Allen Kromholz came to serve the Congregational church.

Riverside Junior High School. Today this is known as Riverside Middle School.

Reverend Kromholz came to minister to the souls of his congregation, but he was also a man of ideals and strong beliefs and one of his beliefs was in open housing and equality for African Americans. He began to pepper his sermons with political themes. His impact on the youth of the church was especially mesmerizing. He encouraged their efforts at creating a newsletter called *Truth* in which they expressed their feelings about the United States and life in Watertown. He also helped to create a coffee house for young people to hang out in. To put it simply, Kromholz was trying to change things too quickly. In Watertown, change does not come without considered thought and a certain degree of kicking and screaming. His involvement in the Civil Rights Movement, plus his meetings and dialogues with young people of the church, which caused them to question their time-honored belief system, was considered by many in the church, including A.E. "Mike" Bentzin who was the city's mayor at the time, to be detrimental. As a result, pressure was placed upon Reverend Kromholz to resign in 1968. The full story of these events are related in the book *Crisis In Watertown* by Lynn Eden, which is considered by many to be a must-read for anyone new to the city.

This entire episode is reminiscent of a case involving an equally charismatic minister, Reverend Christian Sans, the founder of Saint Mark's Lutheran Church. He came here at the request of Germans living in Watertown in 1854 to minister to them. Under his leadership, the new group founded a church and built the first brick house of worship in Jefferson County. But his outspoken ways soon got him into trouble. He preached politics from his pulpit, urged, and even directed at times the way his parishioners should vote in elections, but worse, he was against drinking on the Sabbath and slavery! His actions created a great furor in the city and the German press attacked him with all its might. It got to the point where Sans had to be accompanied by bodyguards whenever he went about in public. The pressure on the church body got to the point that they summoned Sans to a general meeting and he was asked to resign.

In the midst of these goings-on few people realized an event of historic proportions had taken place in Watertown when the final passenger train left the city in 1971. With that final run, over 100 years of rail service to the city came to a close. Railroads had begun to experience a decline in ridership as the use of automobiles increased. After World War II, rail traffic received a further blow as commercial airlines began to increase in prominence. The remaining passenger lines were federalized under Amtrak in 1971 and, as a result, the trains didn't stop

The First Congregational Church. This church was the scene of troubles in the late 1960s due in part to a minister who wished to bring about changes in thinking too quickly.

in Watertown any longer. Trains still pass through the city, and for a few months in 1998, Amtrak ran an experimental passenger service through Watertown, but as of this writing, the era of passenger rail in Watertown is a thing of the past.

The high-water mark of the decade came in 1976, when Watertown and the nation celebrated the bicentennial of the United States. The year-long national celebration culminated in the city with a grand parade, historical displays, and the publication of *Watertown Remembered*, the first book-length history of the city written by the late Professor E.C. Kiessling. Thus, two important decades drew to a close.

Watertown Skyline. This 1970 photograph shows the city more than 30 years ago. (Watertown Historical Society collection.)

12. New Beginnings: 1980–2001

A city of promotion-minded retailers. Watertown . . . a small but thriving industrial complex. Watertown . . . A good place to work and play . . . This is Watertown, our town. A good place to live . . . We like it here.

Watertown Chamber of Commerce Promotional Booklet

The 1980s began in Watertown with a sudden interest in space. Outer space, that is. Everyone had marveled at the first moonwalk, but the citizens of Watertown never thought that they would have a personal stake in space exploration in the person of Daniel Brandenstein, a Watertown boy.

In 1983, Brandenstein, a 1961 graduate of Watertown Senior High School, and a crew of astronauts flew into space. This mission was the very first night launch of a space shuttle. In 1985, Brandenstein also flew as a member of the crew of the *Discovery* mission. He visited space again in 1990 on a *Columbia* mission and finally on the maiden voyage of the space shuttle *Endeavour* in 1992. All in all, Brandenstein put in 789 hours in space, a record he holds among space shuttle astronauts. He retired from NASA in 1992 and was given a hero's reception in Watertown the same year. A city park in Watertown bears his name.

There was also a sudden interest at this time in historic preservation. This came about as a result of the loss of several historic buildings on Main Street, most notably the Valley Bank building. This structure was erected in 1896 by the Wiggenhorn Cigar Company and was a distinctive local landmark with its Moorish copper tower. In 1985, it and the Kusel Hardware Store building next to it were demolished to make way for a modern bank building. Citizens tried to reason with the bank officials and get them to reconsider tearing down the buildings, but their pleas fell on deaf ears.

Fearful that Watertown could lose its entire architectural heritage, the city enacted a historic preservation ordinance in 1987. This was met with great opposition, but the ordinance did put a halt to wide-scale destruction and inappropriate "re-muddling" of historic buildings. As a footnote to the story of the Valley Bank, it is with a certain amount of satisfaction to note that the M&I Bank absorbed the Valley Bank in the 1990s and, in 1995, this new bank building was put on the market. Today, it is home to the Lebanon State Bank.

Among the many things the newly created Historical Preservation Commission did was aid in the creation of the River Walkway, a wooden boardwalk that lines the eastern bank of the Rock River. Stretching from the Main Street bridge southward to Milwaukee Street, the walkway has proven to be a popular spot for pedestrians and tourists in the downtown area. A continuation of the existing boardwalk is being planned.

In 1987, the city celebrated another milestone in its history when Watertown held its Sesquicentennial Celebration, marking the 150th anniversary of the city's founding. A year-long series of historical articles, a grand parade, and contests, culminating with live music and other festivities at Riverside Park marked this event. The Riverside Park celebration has since grown into a yearly event known as Riverfest, which attracts live musical acts and draws thousands to Watertown in August each year.

Pity that the city chose to celebrate the anniversary a year late once again.

The final years of the twentieth century saw many changes in Watertown. For example, in 1991, the city instituted a 911 emergency service; curbside recycling was established throughout the city in 1994; and in order to come to grips with the ever expanding city boundaries, a second postal code, 53098, was added in 1993, which separated the Dodge County portion of the city from the Jefferson County portion.

Watertown again answered its nation's call by sending its young men off to the Persian Gulf in 1990 when war broke out. Watertown suffered one casualty, Patrick Wanke, in this conflict.

As this book is being written, another war has broken out, a war on terrorism that was brought about by the cowardly attacks on the United States. On September 11, 2001, two planes loaded with innocent American passengers struck the World Trade Center in New York City. How this all will end is uncertain.

As the 1990s began to slip away, the city was in turmoil. Things left unattended to for years, like the resurfacing and repair of the city streets, now cried out to be seen to; longtime Watertown industries closed their doors for good, throwing hundreds of people out of work; and everyone was left to wonder, "Where will it all end?"

The downtown business district, long neglected in favor of the retail developments on South Church Street, suffered greatly during this period. In the early days of the 1980s, a new shopping center, Watertown Square, opened, taking still more stores away from the downtown area, and with the opening of Wal-Mart in 1992 and the opening of an outlet mall in nearby Johnson Creek in 1998, more and more consumers were being siphoned away from the heart of the city. But the drawing power of Main Street is still strong and, in 1998, Walgreen's Drugs opened a large store at the head of the street, followed in 1999 by Hollywood Video, which opened a mini-shopping center across the street from it. Another draw to downtown Watertown is the Market, a specialty shopping mall created in a former lumberyard in 1995. These businesses have done a great deal to enhance the downtown business district.

CAPTAIN DANIEL BRANDENSTEIN. A Watertown city park is named for this record-holding local astronaut.

In 1998, in an effort to tap into the city's tourism potential, the Watertown Tourism Board was created. To date, this board has been responsible for establishing a city tourism web site, creating a brochure that points out the city's advantages as a tourist destination, and it has also been responsible for the many colorful murals that dot Main Street. These murals, painted by local artists, depict various aspects of Watertown's rich culture and history. In 1999, the city was named to the national Main Street Program and this, together with the efforts of the Historic Preservation Commission and the Tourism Board, has caused downtown business owners to begin to appreciate the history and charm of their buildings. This is an exciting time for Watertown as its citizens are witnessing a rebirth of their Main Street.

Other civic improvements that occurred within the last years of the twentieth century included the creation of a new aquatic center and the communal construction of a playground area for the children of Watertown. The former Watertown Municipal Swimming Pool was one of the last projects to be built under Roosevelt's WPA program and it satisfied Watertown residents for over 50 years. The building of the pool gave much-needed jobs to men and insured that the residents of the city would have a safe place to swim. Previously, recreational bathing took place in the Rock River at a municipal beach located along East

DANIEL KUSEL'S HARDWARE STORE. This is an early view, c. 1870, of the store that was a mainstay on Main Street from 1849 to 1985.

Division Street. This "swimming hole" provided pleasure for many until the water in this spot got too polluted for swimming purposes. The new pool opened in June 1942 amidst a celebration and served the city until 1993 when, faced with the prospect of massive repairs to the existing pool, the city decided to build a grand aquatic center, complete with a massive waterslide. After intensive fundraising efforts, the Watertown Aquatic Center was dedicated and thrown open to the residents of the city on June 4, 1993. Following on the heels of this came Chamberland, which was a city-wide cooperative effort to build a safe child's play area. Located in Riverside Park, Chamberland opened in 1996.

Something else began to happen during the 1980s and 1990s. A new ethnic group began to rise in prominence, the Hispanic-American community. According to figures reported in the magazine *Channel: A Newsletter of the Wisconsin Division for Libraries, Technology, and Community Learning* in 2001, Watertown had the sixth highest percentage increase in Hispanic population since 1990, at 318 percent. Churches began to offer Spanish services, the Watertown Public Library has begun the construction of a special Spanish section of books for Hispanic patrons, and for a time in the latter half of the 1990s, there was a rash of Spanish-themed and -run retail stores on Main Street. The German element is still in evidence and one has only to scan the Watertown telephone book to see how many descendants of Watertown's German settlers still live here, but times have certainly changed.

But all of this seeming prosperity has not stopped the closing of factories and, as stated previously, in the 1990s and in the early years of the twenty-first century, we have lost several longtime industries like the G.B. Lewis Company, known at the last as Allied Molded Plastics, an institution that dated to 1863.

So what is there left to say about Watertown? Well, first of all, it is not a perfect place, but it is a good place to live and to raise one's children. It is a place to retire to and the percentage of senior citizens is growing. And finally, it is a city that has potential. In 2000, the city stood at a population of 21,598, an increase of 12.83 percent, or 2,456 people, since 1990. No one can deny the city's growth. Watertown continues to reinvent itself to suit the times. With luck and guidance, the city should continue to thrive and rise to meet the challenges that the twenty-first century will bring.

There is no better way to end this history than to quote from the Harvest Jubilee and Carnival Souvenir Program of 1899:

> Anyone who has ever lived in Watertown long enough to become acquainted with her beauties and pleasant associations will always carry a warm spot in his heart in memory of her. . . .

A DAY AT THE BEACH. Bathers enjoy a day at the Watertown Municipal Bathing Beach, c. 1920.

BIBLIOGRAPHY

Official Program and Souvenir [of the] Harvest Jubilee and Carnival. Watertown, 1899.

Blumenfeld, Ralph D. *Home Town.* London: Hutchinson & Company, Ltd., 1944.

Colonius, H.C. "Geschichte von Watertown, nach mundlichen Uberliefungen." Serially in *Watertown Weltburger* beginning 26 September 1868. Repeated serially in same newspaper beginning 15 April 1905.

Eden, Lynn. *Crisis in Watertown, The Polarization of an American Community.* Ann Arbor, MI: University of Michigan Press, 1972.

Feld, Reuben A. *Notes, Quotes and Anecdotes of Watertown.* Watertown: privately printed.

Gurda, John. "Commuter Trains Have Rich History Here." *Milwaukee Journal Sentinel.* 3 May 1998.

Holmes, Fred L. *Old World Wisconsin, Around Europe in the Badger State.* Eau Claire, WI: E.M. Hale Company, 1944.

Jacobi, C. Hugo. "Reminiscences of Early Days in Watertown." Serially in *Watertown Daily Times,* beginning 1 February 1924. Original articles in German in *Watertown Weltburger* beginning 5 May 1923.

Jeanson, Jill. "Vegetation Study of Tivoli Island." Unpublished research paper in collections at the Watertown Historical Society, 1975.

Johnson, Timothy. "Letter to John Brownell." Collection of the Watertown Historical Society, 4 September 1845.

Kiessling, Elmer C. *Watertown Remembered.* Watertown: Franklin Publishers Inc. for the Watertown Historical Society, 1976.

Killian, Marcella. *Watertown, Wisconsin Centennial 1854–1954.* Watertown: 1954.

Lord, A.I. *Industrial Review of Watertown, Wisconsin.* Milwaukee: Published by A.I Lord, January 1897.

Ott, John Henry, ed. *Jefferson County, Wisconsin and Its People.* Two volumes. Chicago: S.J. Clarke Publishing Company, 1917.

Quiner, E.B. *City of Watertown, Wisconsin: Its Manufacturing & Railroad Advantages & Business Statistics.* Watertown: 1856.

Rausch, Joan and Carol Lohry Cartwright. *City of Watertown, Wisconsin Architectural and Historical Intensive Survey Report 1986–1987.* LaCrosse, WI: Architectural Researches Inc., August 1987.

Schaefer, Joseph, trans. and ed. *Intimate Letters of Carl Schurz.* Madison, WI: State Historical Society of Wisconsin, 1929.
Swart, Hannah Werwath. *Koshkonong Country Revisited, Volume One.* Muskego, WI: Marek Lithographics, Inc., 1981.
Watertown Chronicle, 30 June 1847–9 October 1856.
Watertown Daily Times, 23 November 1895–Present.
Watertown Democratic State Register, 12 March 1850–4 November 1854.
Watertown Gazette, 22 July 1879–18 March 1937.
Watertown Republican, 24 April 1867–6 April 1906 .

THE GONDOLIER SKATING CLUB, 1925. Watertown residents have long enjoyed getting out on the ice in the winters. (Arline Hildebrandt collection.)

INDEX

BEALS AND PRATT SHOE COMPANY. This 1920s photo shows the interior of one of several of Watertown's shoe factories, this one on South Water Street. (Watertown Historical Society collection.)

WATERTOWN SKYLINE, EARLY 1990S. Watertown, in the words of a Chamber of Commerce booster book, is "a good place to live. We like it here." (Watertown Daily Times.)